Praise for Richard Russo's

The Destiny Thief

"It turns out that Russo the nonfiction writer is a lot like Russo the Pulitzer Prize–winning novelist. He is affably disagreeable, wry, idiosyncratic, vulnerably bighearted, a craftsman of lubricated sentences. . . . Perhaps what's most admirable about these essays is their genial and searching tone."

—*The New York Times Book Review*

"A heartfelt exploration of [Russo's] life as a writer." —PopSugar

"More than a few wise reflections on the craft of writing."

—*Southern Living*

"Masterful. . . . Wonderfully candid." —*Tulsa Book Review*

"A remarkable and insightful exploration into the mind of a wonderful writer." —Bookreporter

"All-encompassing. . . . Anyone in search of an eye-opening series of essays by a distinguished writer about writing and the writing life need look no further." —*The National Book Review*

RICHARD RUSSO

The Destiny Thief

Richard Russo is the author of eight novels, most recently *Every-body's Fool* and *That Old Cape Magic*; two collections of stories; and the memoir *Elsewhere*. In 2002 he received the Pulitzer Prize for *Empire Falls*, which, like *Nobody's Fool*, was adapted to film in a multiple award-winning HBO miniseries; in 2016 he was given the Indie Champion Award by the American Booksellers Association; and in 2017 he received France's Grand Prix de Littérature Américaine. He lives in Portland, Maine.

Richard Russo is available for select speaking engagements. To inquire about a possible speaking appearance, please contact Penguin Random House Speakers Bureau at speakers@penguinrandomhouse.com or visit www.prhspeakers.com.

The Destiny Thief

The Destiny Thief

Essays on Writing, Writers and Life

RICHARD RUSSO

VINTAGE BOOKS

A Division of Penguin Random House LLC

New York

Contents

The Destiny Thief

The Destiny Thief

As a writer, you aren't anybody until you become somebody.

—James Salter

I am the same man I was when I was a struggling nobody . . . still a writer trying to find his way through a maze. Should I be anything else?

—Raymond Chandler

Some time ago I had a lengthy telephone conversation with a man I'll call David. I'd known him nearly forty years earlier at the University of Arizona, where we shared a fiction workshop taught by the writer Robert C. S. Downs, who encouraged both of us, but David especially. At the time I was finishing up my PhD in American literature, so when I asked Downs about taking a workshop, I assumed he'd put me in one at the graduate level, but he didn't. My prose, he explained, was full of jargon and intellectual pretension. Most writers had about a thousand pages of shitty prose in them, he went on, and these have to be expelled before they can hope to write seriously. "In your case," he added, "make it two thousand." And so, pushing thirty, I swallowed my pride and enrolled in a workshop full of twenty-year-olds, many of whom were better writers than I was.

David was working on a novel about a rock-and-roll band, and having once played in a band myself, I was envious of both his subject matter and his bold talent and even more jealous of the fact that at age twenty he'd already figured out what he wanted to do with his life, whereas I'd wasted the better part of a decade pursuing an advanced degree I no longer really wanted. What I didn't know about David was what a rough time he was having outside the classroom. His mother, whom he'd dearly loved, had recently died of cancer, and his father was an emotional tyrant. David himself had very little money and was drinking heavily. Indeed, the fiction workshop—his dream of becoming a novelist one day—was just about all that was holding him together. Then, near the end of the semester, he got in trouble, courtesy of his poet girlfriend. She'd been assigned six poems, and the day before they were due she hadn't written a single line. When she told David she was thinking about dropping the course, he said, "Nonsense. We'll write them now. How hard can it be?" So they sat down and did just that, the girlfriend writing three poems, David the other three.

They both thought the results were pretty good, but the girlfriend was unprepared for the praise lavished on the poems, in particular the one David had written about his mother. After class, she made the mistake of confiding to a classmate that all of the poems had been written the night before, half of them by her boyfriend. When her friend reported the infraction, both she and David were hauled before Downs, the director of creative writing, to explain themselves. The girlfriend arrived at the meeting determined to defend the work as her own. David, they agreed beforehand, would admit only to offering advice. But this wasn't Downs's first experience with academic dishonesty, and instead of asking if she'd written the poems in question, he quoted the best line from the whole batch of poems and asked if she'd written it; she immediately broke down.

Since she'd come clean and it was her first offense, Downs said he'd recommend a D in the course but no mark on her record. He then turned to his star fiction writer and said, "Good poems." David sighed, accepting the compliment, proud to have written the line that his mentor so admired, but fearful of what came next. The dishonesty charge was the least of it, he confessed. He was out of money and about to be evicted from the shithole where he was living. He'd dropped the rest of his courses earlier in the term, and though he hated the idea, there was nothing to do but return home in defeat. He hadn't intended to tell Downs any of this, but there he was, spilling his guts about how much the workshop meant to him and how much he hated the idea of not completing it. When he asked what his grade would be, Downs said he'd be getting the A he'd earned and added, perhaps to bolster his spirits, that it would likely be the only one in the class. Apparently we were not a stellar group. "What about Rick?" David asked. After all, I was a grad student. Downs shrugged. "Rick doesn't want to be a writer. He wants to be a teacher." (He was wrong about that, but he couldn't have known. After getting the PhD, I did plan on applying for teaching positions.)

Now fast-forward to 2002. For both David and me a lot has happened. He's eventually finished his undergraduate degree, then gone on to graduate school for an MFA in poetry, not fiction.

He has married, had kids, is teaching college to support his writing habit and has become middle-aged. He's continued to struggle periodically with alcohol but remained functional, enjoyed success as a poet and become something of a legend among his students. Along the way he's finished that rock-and-roll novel, but frustrated by his inability to find an agent, finally published it himself. Maybe his life isn't the one he imagined back in Tucson, but for the most part he's been pretty happy.

Until one day he picks up the University of Arizona alumni magazine and discovers that a student from his undergraduate workshop (who did indeed get a B) has been awarded the Pulitzer Prize for fiction. According to the article, the prizewinner taught for a while before quitting to write full-time. David feels something inside him come untethered—and really, who could blame him? Somehow he and I have swapped destinies. He is the teacher, I the writer. He wants someone to explain the cosmic mechanism by which such a cruel joke could be perpetrated. In fact, he'd like *me* to explain.

As if I'd know.

I've written a lot about destiny in my fiction, not because I understand it, but because I'd like to. If David was puzzled by the narrative arc of our lives, he wasn't alone. At the risk of sounding falsely modest, I have to say I'm not aware of anyone—teacher, family member, friend—who predicted anything like the great good fortune that has befallen me in the writing career that I came to fairly late. Some years ago I ran into an old girlfriend who said she'd been following my work with both pleasure and mystification. "I always thought you were a nice enough guy," she told me, clearly trying to puzzle it through and not wanting to hurt my feelings, "but I never dreamed you had *books* in you." I know exactly how she felt. I can't explain it even now. Anyone who's interested in my early life can have a look at my memoir *Elsewhere,* though for the purposes of this discussion a thumbnail sketch will suffice. I lived the first eighteen years of my life in Gloversville, a poor mill town in upstate New York. Raised Catholic, I was for many years an altar boy. My parents separated when I was a kid, so I was brought up by my nervous mother, who hated where we lived, and by my grandparents, who owned the house we lived in. If my mother was adamant about anything, it was that, as an American, I could be whatever I wanted to be. That I was as good as anybody. I was always to remember this in case anyone had the temerity to suggest otherwise.

My mostly absent father had come to a whole different set of conclusions. He was part of the Normandy invasion and returned from the war with a personal philosophy that fit neatly onto his favorite coffee mug, which I still have: HERE'S TO YOU AS GOOD AS YOU ARE AND HERE'S TO ME, AS BAD AS I AM, BUT AS GOOD AS YOU ARE AND AS BAD AS I AM, I'M AS GOOD AS YOU ARE, AS BAD AS I AM. It was, now that I think about it, the joke version of my mother's mantra, and to complete this gag the mug's handle was on the *inside* of the cylinder. Call it an object lesson: that being as good as anybody might not be of much use if you had to go through life with a basic design flaw. For my father, being born poor was just such a flaw. Having a name that ended in a vowel was another.

But never mind, my mother said. In addition to America, she believed in education and its ability to negate any of these flaws.

My high school was tiny, and without expending much effort I flourished there. I had enough of my father's easy charm to talk most people into giving me what I wanted; and on the others I could employ my mother's tidal persistence, her innate ability to nick away at people until they gave me what I was after, just to be rid of me. The University of Arizona was twice the size of my hometown, though, and what a rude awakening that was. My first day there I went to the registrar's office, hoping to do something out of sequence, probably register early for classes, and was met by a grim woman who sized me up at a glance. Holding up a hand to stop me midexplanation, she said, "Have you matriculated?" The question stopped me cold. I didn't want to admit I had no idea what the word meant. Her tone made it sound rather personal, almost sexual, but that couldn't be, could it? I had a fifty-fifty chance of being right, though, so I said no, not recently, but I was willing to if it was strictly necessary. *Tomorrow,* I was told sternly. I was a *freshman* and would matriculate with the rest of my class tomorrow and not before. What I was asking for, she explained, was special treatment, and I wasn't going to get it, not from her.

My roommate that first semester was a boy from a tiny Arizona mining town that he was clearly homesick for already, less than twenty-four hours after leaving it. He couldn't tell me enough about the place, which was apparently perfect in every respect. He seemed to have little interest in his classes, and as the semester wore on he had a devil of a time making friends. He wanted to pledge a fraternity, but none would have him. Back home he had a girlfriend, but at the university the girls he asked out gave him the once-over and said no in a way that made him understand he was wrong to have asked. At first he did poorly in his classes, which seemed to surprise him, but then he did worse; finally the dean of students requested an interview, at which it was decided that he'd be happier at a junior college closer to home. I was glad when he left and not just because it meant I'd have our room to myself for the rest of the term; in the brief time we'd shared it, I'd come to loathe him viscerally, though at the time I didn't understand why. Now it couldn't be clearer. Looking at him, his face alive with angry zits, was like looking in the mirror.

And so, badly shaken and far from home, I set about developing a strategy for surviving at an institution determined to make me understand that while I might be as good as anybody, I was certainly no better. The gist of my plan was this: I would (1) pretend to know things I didn't rather than risk the humiliation of ignorance and (2) conceal, as far as humanly possible, who I was and where I came from. I'd figure out what I was supposed to like and admire, and would do so even when I didn't. In other words, I would lie through my teeth about everything. Fortunately, I wasn't the only liar there. College is, after all, where we go to reinvent ourselves, to sever our ties with the past, to become the person we always wanted to be and were prevented from being by people who knew better. Actually, none of this is quite as bad as it sounds. Many years later, giving a commencement address at the college from which my younger daughter was graduating, I would compare going to college to entering the witness-protection program. You're *supposed* to try on a new identity or two. Indeed, it would not only defeat the purpose, it would be downright dangerous to leave the program easily recognizable as the person who'd entered it.

Anyway, I changed. I took my classes more seriously than

I'd done in high school, not out of any abstract love of learning but rather because the competition was stiffer, and I figured the more I actually knew, the less I'd have to pretend to know. I ditched all the "stylish" clothes I'd brought with me from the East and dressed in western jeans with button flies. I had to be taught that these worked better if you buttoned from the bottom up, not from the top down. There was a lot to learn, but I was gradually able to blend in. When asked where I was from, I substituted "upstate New York" for "Gloversville," a deft maneuver that allowed me to trade embarrassment over my origins, a new experience, for guilt, which, having been raised Catholic, I was used to. Summers, when I returned to Gloversville to work road construction with my father, were the toughest. Because in truth I was very happy to be back home and living in the house where I'd grown up, where people knew the old me. I hadn't realized just how much I loved my grandparents until I saw them again that first summer, and in their company I felt the sting of my dogged efforts at reinvention out west. I began to understand that in denying where I was from, I was also denying them and the many sacrifices they'd made for my mother and me.

I'd made my choice, though, and there was no going back. I was becoming someone else. Someone better. However high the cost, I'd pay it.

In the late seventies, just as I was completing my PhD, the market for academics went into the tank. The first year, I went job hunting with my friend Kevin McIlvoy, who had, if memory serves, three interviews; I had just one. Even though the rooms were discounted, we couldn't afford to stay in the MLA convention hotels. Indeed, we could barely pay for the gas it took to get there. That Christmas my wife bought me a tweed jacket so I'd look the part when presenting myself as a scholar. Mc thought his interviews went well, but at some point on the long drive home, the same realization dawned on both of us—that in order for either of us to be offered the jobs we'd applied for, all the flights carrying other applicants home to Stanford and Princeton and Ann Arbor and Berkeley would have to crash. What troubled me almost as much as *not* getting the job I'd interviewed for was the remote—okay, extremely remote—possibility that I actually might. I'd managed to publish three chapters from my dissertation on the early American novelist Charles Brockden Brown, which almost made up for my dubious state-university pedigree. At the end of my interview, the department chair shook my hand and told me he was impressed that I was publishing so significantly right out of the gate. "If we offer you the position," he said, "you'll be our man in Charles Brockden Brown." No doubt he meant this as a compliment, but my blood ran cold because by then I'd pretty much quit scholarship. And when someone with better credentials backed out at the last minute, I'd been offered the last slot in Arizona's MFA program. I was feverishly writing fiction now, pumping out story after story, though I hadn't published anything yet. I'd also begun work on a novel.

I needn't have worried, of course. None of the flights carrying real scholars back to Harvard and Columbia crashed, and I wasn't offered the job. Which meant I had one final year to finish my stalled dissertation and make myself into a writer. Could I do that? Sure. Why not?

————

Here's a short inventory of what I'd learned by the time I left the University of Arizona in 1980, with an MFA in fiction and a PhD in American literature. I knew:

> quite a lot about the nineteenth-century novel, Twain and Dickens in particular.
>
> less about the twentieth century, very little about the eighteenth.
>
> enough about Gass, Elkin, Barthelme, Coover, Vonnegut and the other postmoderns to know they didn't speak to me.
>
> how to create characters that, for the most part, rang true.
>
> that it's conflict, more than plot, that drives the best stories forward.
>
> that characters had to speak out of their own need, not their author's.
>
> the ins and outs of point of view.

I also half knew a few other things. For instance, I had a theoretical understanding of tone—that it represents the writer's attitude toward his material, and that I wasn't going to be any good until I'd mastered its practice.

Before leaving Arizona, I gave my just-completed novel—set in Tucson—to Downs, who'd continued to encourage me despite his unshakable belief that I would end up an academic. I was hoping to be told I was wrong, that the book was good, but deep down I knew it wasn't, and so I wasn't surprised by his verdict that the book was mostly inert. What knocked the stuffing out of me, though, was what he considered its silver lining. There was, he said, one short section, about forty pages of backstory set in a small upstate New York mill town, that came vividly to life. "You know that world," he told me. Even now I remember how the blood rushed to my face and roared in my ears. "Not really," I told the man who'd been kind enough to read my novel and tell me the truth about it. "I made that all up." I mean, come on. What did he think I was, a rube?

Better, I thought, to be somebody's man in Charles Brockden Brown.

My first academic posting was at a branch campus of Penn State University, where I taught what everybody in the English depart-ment did—a ton of freshman composition and the occasional lit course designed to keep us from swallowing the entire bottle of amphetamines instead of just the one or two required to keep us grading papers deep into the night. My lit-class syllabus that first year was made up entirely of books I'd taught before. Not very adventurous, but I could use the time saved for writing stories. One night, preparing for my morning class on Steinbeck, I came across the following passage in *Cannery Row*:

> Up in back of the vacant lot is . . . the stern and stately whore house of Dora Flood; a decent, clean, honest, old-fashioned sporting house where a man can take a glass of beer among friends. This is no fly-by-night clip-joint but a sturdy, virtuous club, built, maintained and disciplined by Dora who, madam and girl for fifty years, has through the exercise of special gifts of tact and honesty, charity and a certain realism, made her-self respected by the intelligent, the learned, and the kind. And by the same token she is hated by the twisted and lascivi-

ous sisterhood of married spinsters whose husbands respect the home but don't like it very much.

Dora is a great woman, a great big woman with flaming orange hair and a taste for Nile green evening dresses.

I pause here, because that's where I ground to a halt at the time, dumbstruck, my jaw open on a hinge. How had I not seen it before? As I said earlier, I understood that "tone" was a writer's attitude toward his subject matter, but I somehow hadn't imagined how this attitude might manifest itself in actual language. Dora Flood, we're told, is a great woman. The word "great," used to modify a noun, seems to convey a value judgment about her character. Except Dora's supposed greatness is immediately undermined by "a great big woman," and suddenly "great" modifies not a noun but another adjective, "big," and the meaning pivots slyly. We're no longer talking about Dora's moral attributes, but rather her physical size. Further, her "taste for Nile green evening dresses" to offset her bright orange hair actually suggests a lack of taste. The words say one thing but mean another. Lurking somewhere in the rhetorical shadows is an authorial presence, a disembodied voice, and it's tempting to identify that voice as Steinbeck's until we remember *The Grapes of Wrath* and *The Red Pony*, where the voice is different, more earnest, less playful. It's not so much *the* John Steinbeck we sense behind the curtain as *a* John Steinbeck, the author in a particular mood, chosen specifically for the material at hand.

I'd been told before that writers had to have two identities: their real-life one—who they are with their spouses and colleagues and friends—as well as another, who they *become* when they sit down to write. This second identity, I now saw, was fluid, as changeable as the weather, as unfixed as our emotions. As readers, we naturally expect novels to introduce us to a new cast of characters and dramatic events, but could it also be that the writer has to reinvent *himself* for the purpose of telling each new story? If he's free to invent a different voice for each new book, then which is his true one? And how is it remotely fair for Steinbeck to possess so many voices when I, even after dutifully expelling my two thousand pages of wretched prose, still didn't have a single one?

What pissed me off even more than this glaring inequity was that the voice Steinbeck used in *Cannery Row* was so damnably familiar. I'd heard it many times before—and not in any book, either. The wry insistence that we understand Dora's establishment isn't a *whore house* so much as a *sporting house*? That what goes on there could actually be construed as *virtuous*? That people who object to prostitution are small-minded? Outside of *Cannery Row,* where had I heard conventional morality mocked so winningly? Who else in my experience had cunningly insinuated that there was more than one kind of *charity*? Who, back when I was an altar boy, had demanded of me *a certain realism* when it came to moral matters? How was it, I asked myself, that John Steinbeck was suddenly speaking to me *in my own father's voice,* a voice that, once I'd recognized it, I felt every bit as entitled to as his signature widow's peak. This wasn't a voice I'd have to imitate, as I'd tried to do with Salinger and Twain and Raymond Chandler. It was already mine. Or it would be if I could grow into it. But how?

That evening, I dug out the novel I hadn't looked at since leaving Arizona and reread the forty pages Downs had liked. He'd been right, of course, damn his hide. Like it or not, I *did* really know this mill town, and now I saw what I'd missed earlier—that there was no reason a whole novel shouldn't be set there. What I'd thought of as my novel's backstory *was* the story, but I just hadn't let it be. They weren't exactly good, those forty pages, but they were mine, which was more than could be said for the other two hundred.

This should've been good news, right? Wasn't it the break-through every writer longs for? For the last year I'd been churn-ing out stories and sending them to magazines as diverse as *The New Yorker* and *Mademoiselle* and *Ellery Queen's Mystery Magazine*. And to what purpose? What I'd wanted was for editors to like and admire me, never suspecting the simple truth that as yet there was no me to like, much less to admire. Now I could set aside all that silly striving and get down to the real business of becoming a writer.

So, why did those forty pages cause my spirits to plummet? Why, for the first time, did I feel like giving up? No doubt part of my despair had to do with the magnitude of the mistake I'd been faithful to for so long. Over the last twelve months or so, a few of my stories had been accepted by little magazines, and main-stream editors sometimes added short notes—*Try us again*—at the bottom of their rejection letters. I'd allowed this evidence to convince me that I was becoming a better writer, that I was *close*, whereas now I saw clearly that I was just becoming more skilled, more sure-handed with my tools, which isn't the same thing. I wasn't close at all. Discovering who I was as a writer might be the final piece of the puzzle, but it also sent me back to the beginning. Yesterday, before visiting Dora Flood's whorehouse, I had a dozen stories ready to send out to magazines, each one representing the break I'd been longing for. Now I understood they all belonged in the trash. If, armed with my newfound identity, I went right back to work, it might be a year or more before I had anything to show anybody. Close? This was starting over.

Nor was that the worst. Sure, rereading those forty pages, seeing their potential, had been exhilarating, but it was also dispiriting. If at long last I'd found not just my material but also the voice I'd need to bring it into sharp focus, did it necessarily follow that the result would be a book anybody wanted to read? Okay, great, I'd discovered a "me," but it was the same low-rent mill-town "me" I'd been fleeing ever since I left Gloversville. The new me I'd hoped to discover in Arizona was more like Dickens's me or Cheever's or Ross Macdonald's. They all had a *good* me, the lucky bastards. My me sucked. Earlier in the semester, when my department chair in far-off State College somehow got wind of the fact that I was writing stories instead of doing research, he warned me to quit. I'd been hired as a scholar, not a fiction writer, and by ignoring my scholarship I was endangering my chances for tenure and promotion. Though I all but told him to go fuck himself, now I wondered if maybe he was right. We were broke, and my wife was pregnant with our second child, so maybe it was time to forget trying to become someone I really wasn't and settle for being somebody's man in Charles Brockden Brown. That, at least, was a living.

Destiny is forged in moments like these. Curiosity and discovery in Manichaean balance with despair and self-loathing. Writing, like life itself, is difficult. Many truly talented people give up every day.

The publication of my first novel, *Mohawk,* whose origin was those flawed pages that Downs liked, got me my first job as a writer at Southern Illinois University. There, in Carbondale, I also had the great good fortune to meet and become fast friends with the poet Rodney Jones. He hailed from Alabama, and his background—small town, lower-middle class—was similar to my own. Rodney seemed as surprised as I was to have had some success doing something so different from what had been expected of him. SIU was very much a blue-collar campus, which suited us fine. We were both committed not only to our craft but also to our student writers, many of them first-generation college students, as well as to the program we'd been given free rein to develop. Most semesters we had students in common and gossiped about them—who was writing what, who showing real promise—like a couple of matrons over a clothesline. One beery Friday afternoon, Rodney was singing the praises of a young poet while I was of my best fiction writer, only to shortly discover we were talking about the same person. He'd come to the university over the objections of his family, none of whom had ever been out of the tiny Ohio River town he was writing about, and all of whom saw education as a waste of time and money. He was quiet and seemed to have few friends, and by snooping around in his academic records we discovered he hadn't distinguished himself in his other classes. Indeed, as the term progressed we began getting worried notes from other professors that he was in danger of flunking their courses. But he wrote poetry *and* prose as if his hands were on fire.

Though I don't think it occurred to us at the time, Rodney and I probably both saw a lot of ourselves—Rodney's rural Alabama and my upstate New York—in what he was writing. We each took him aside to let him know his talent was rare and it was our job to help him nurture it if that's what he wanted. As a junior, his stories and poems were good enough to get him into the best MFA programs in the country. We even offered to go to bat for him with his more doubtful professors, for whom, he freely admitted, he hadn't worked nearly so hard, caring nothing for the subjects they taught. More than anything, he seemed genuinely baffled that we were so interested in him. Nobody else ever had been. Were we idiots? Then, near the end of the term, he vanished—from our classes, from the dorm, from campus. A family emergency, we thought, since he'd notified no one that he was leaving. Except he never returned. We assumed he'd simply flunked out. Without any real justification, Rodney and I gave him incompletes so as to leave the door open.

One morning that summer Rodney appeared at my door, suggesting a road trip. Still troubled by our student's disappearance, he'd gone to the registrar's office and gotten his parents' address in their Ohio River town, and that's where we found him, working in a dilapidated video store. He apologized for leaving without saying goodbye and thanked us for the interest we'd shown in his work. But no, he said, he wouldn't be coming back. His mind was made up. Was it a question of money? we inquired. Because we could help with scholarships and other forms of financial aid. No, he insisted, it wasn't really about money. He just didn't think he'd be writing anymore. Clearly, our presence there—in this video store, in the town he'd written about so vividly—made him anxious, so in the end there was nothing for us to do but leave.

On the drive home, Rodney and I came to the same reluctant conclusion. Our fear had been that it was his other professors, his failures in *their* classes, that had caused him to leave the university, whereas he'd actually left because of us. He was used to the poor opinion of others. He'd always been expected to fail. To him failure was a warm embrace, as familiar and reassuring as his family and the grungy little town he'd spent his whole life in. What Rodney and I were offering him was an entirely different narrative, one he must have yearned for at some level or else he never would have gone to college to begin with, but up close it was so terrifying that he'd fled. Now he was suffering the kind of embarrassment you feel when you flirt with a pretty girl who, for reasons you can't fathom, flirts back. Since she's clearly out of your league, she's either toying with you or has temporarily gone crazy. Later, when she gets a better look at you and returns to her senses, she'll send you packing. Better to send yourself packing before you fall in love, before you become so lost you'll never find your way home. What will haunt you, though, maybe forever, is the possibility that you were wrong about her, which in effect means that maybe you were wrong about yourself.

Okay, I've been coy here, and it's time to come clean. At the beginning of this essay I mentioned my telephone conversation with David, and you must've wondered why he called me after so long. Actually, he explained, it wasn't his first call. Since reading about me in that alumni magazine, he'd rung me several times, though, with one notable exception, he always hung up quickly when I or my wife answered. The exception was when he drunk-dialed me in the middle of the night after watching the three-and-a-half-hour HBO miniseries of *Empire Falls*, with only a bottle of whiskey for company. He had every intention of congratulating me on my success, he said, but then suddenly was spouting nasty, spiteful things and slammed the phone down before I could reply.

Anyway, he was calling again to explain how long he'd blamed me for stealing his destiny and to apologize for all those hang ups and especially for the late-night call when he'd read me the riot act. He clearly needed to say all this, so I didn't respond until he was finished. It was probably true that he owed someone an apology, I conceded, but whoever he'd called and berated in the middle of the night, it wasn't me. My memory isn't great, but I would've remembered that. What made me feel bad was that I'd been in his head for so long, an unwelcome and unhealthy presence, causing him unnecessary grief and self-doubt. We ended the call on a good footing. "You mean I didn't have to make this confession?" he chuckled. "I could've gotten away with it?" Everything was forgiven, if indeed there was anything to forgive.

Yet, since then I haven't been able to put him out of my mind, just as I've been unable to forget the gifted student I shared with Rodney Jones. I've never believed that writers are special people with special gifts, but writing isn't easy. Most people who want to be writers end up abandoning the struggle. Who knows why others slog on endlessly against reason and all the odds? I can only tell you why *I* did, and I do so here only because to me the reason still seems completely counterintuitive. That night when I came close to giving up, fearing that I was saddled with a third-rate artistic "me," I didn't give it one last shot because I imagined the result would be success. My mother's mantra to the contrary, I no longer believed, if I ever had, that I could be anything I wanted. I just thought—and in these exact words—*Fuck it.* If the person I was wasn't good enough, fine. If I harbored a basic design flaw (my handle inside the mug) that disqualified me from being a good writer, as lack of speed and athleticism will disqualify you from being the Yankees' center fielder, then so be it. But dear God I was tired of running away, tired of apologizing, tired of trying to figure out what editors and other people wanted. I would make one final attempt so I could be done with writing once and for all. Writing *Mohawk*, my first published novel, felt like an honorable exit strategy. It's tempting to say, in hindsight, that I was beginning to understand that self-consciousness is the enemy of art, but in truth I was just tired of always getting in my own way. I needed not only to claim as my own the very place I'd been fleeing for so long but also to lose myself there, to give my full attention to the kind of people whose lives were, at least to me, both important and essential. And so, with no one left to impress, not even myself, I began, finally, to write.

I'm always surprised by how many writers come from families containing at least one other writer, a fact that might suggest the existence of some "writer gene," though I doubt there is one. Doctors beget doctors, politicians beget politicians and lawyers, alas, lawyers. Why should artists be any different? But the apprentice who has no artistic sibling, father or aunt to observe and consult is, I think, on a particularly perilous and deceptive journey. Most of what an aspiring writer needs to learn—about point of view and plotting and character development and dialogue—is technical and can be learned in workshops such as the one David and I shared in Tucson and that Rodney and I taught in Carbondale. Unfortunately, what can't be taught is absolutely indispensable. A writer's truest self hides in the same dark terrain where self-doubt and anxiety dwell—those dread whisperers—and it's that self they constantly assail. They are, I think, the original hackers, determined to hijack the code, to show us who's boss, to confuse us into thinking the danger comes from without, not from within. Like Odysseus, we have little choice but to lash ourselves to the mast and listen to their Siren song, knowing all too well that they want us on the rocks. There is a narrow passage. There *must* be.

But there's no dead reckoning. We're on our own.

The Gravestone and the Commode

Twenty-five years ago, when my family moved to Waterville, Maine, we bought a house with a finished basement that was sectioned off into a laundry room and a rec room. The latter seemed like the best place for my office, so I soon interred myself there, setting up my desk and computer and half-a-dozen bookcases belowground in a windowless room, where it would be quiet and I wouldn't be underfoot (though I was, of course, literally under the feet of my wife and daughters). I worked in that basement for four years, writing most of my novel *Straight Man* there, before finally putting in a request to come aboveground. The problem was that no one in our family besides me remembered to shut the laundry-room door when the dryer was going, and after a couple loads of towels, the air down there became thick and dry. "I'm asphyxiating," I complained. "I can feel my lungs filling up with lint."

As you may know, requests for exhumation are seldom granted. In all the houses we'd ever lived in during my long academic nomadship, I'd always been relegated to the basement, and this was where my then-teenage daughters had come to believe their father belonged. My wife wasn't thrilled, either. If I was allowed up into the light of day, I might see other things I wanted, and where would it all end? But a movie of my novel *Nobody's Fool* was about to start shooting, and at long last my books were making some money, which meant that for the first time I actually had some juice in the family. Whatever the reason, I unexpectedly prevailed and was allowed to move upstairs into a room whose window looked out onto our backyard, near the center of which stood a gnarled apple tree that bore and then dropped hundreds of hard, green, worm-infested apples each August. This bitter harvest shouldn't have surprised us. Resting against the base of the tree was a gravestone.

When we first moved into the house, I'd briefly puzzled over the stone, especially its inscription:

NIMON KALEEL KATER
Born in Syria, 1897
Died May 11, 1925
Age 28 years

To Western eyes it read like a movie marquee vandalized by children who thought it would be funny to scramble the letters around a little, thereby requiring patrons to rearrange them in order to decide if they wanted to see this movie. I remember squinting at that first name—Nimon—and tracing the N with my index finger on the cold stone, to make sure that was what it was, then conjuring in my warped imagination a fictional encounter between an old stonecutter and his young apprentice, the old man cuffing the kid in the back of the head and shouting, "Not 'Nimon,' you idiot! 'Simon'!" And here the old man would point to the slip of paper upon which his arthritic fingers had scrawled the name his apprentice was supposed to have carved into stone. "Kaleel? What kind of name is Kaleel? I wrote '*Ralph.*'" I mean, the very fact that the stone was resting against our apple tree and marking no apparent grave suggested some sort of error, right? How many reasons can there be for *not* using a gravestone? A sudden change of plans? It turned out to be just a bad cold? Most of the explanations that occurred to me were comic, as were so many of the details on the stone. BORN IN SYRIA, 1897. DIED MAY 11, 1925. How's that for parallelism? When you're born, these lines implied, place is the important thing, so the calendar year's specific enough. When you die, the exact date is the essential piece of information. It doesn't much matter where, one place being as good as another.

My new aboveground work space had formerly been a family room. The previous owners had a hot tub in there, and they must've enjoyed it because they took it with them, leaving behind only its octagonal outline in the carpet. We didn't aspire to a hot tub ourselves, nor did we wish to be reminded of theirs, so we immediately tore up the old soiled carpet and replaced it with a thick beige one of my wife's choosing. "Let's do something about the bathroom while we're at it," she suggested, referring to that tiny cramped space. Since its few square feet of linoleum flooring were in bad shape, we put some leftover beige carpet in there.

Only afterward did I begin to notice that other people's bathrooms are almost never carpeted—for reasons that are fairly obvious, if you think about it, which we hadn't. Bathrooms tend to get wet, with soapy water splashing out of sinks and tubs, while middle-aged men (I don't wish to be indelicate here) invariably lose some of their youthful precision. In a matter of months this wasn't the sort of place we wanted dinner guests to visit between the pasta and main courses. Also, the carpet in my new office was too thick for me to roll around on in my chair, so we decided to cut our losses, tear out the carpet and replace it with tile.

In order to lay the tile, the workers had to remove the commode. They took ours outside and set it out of the way on the back deck while they finished the job. Every time I passed the window, the sight of it cracked me up, planted out there in the open air like an invitation to come clean about things we prefer to keep private. We'd brought in the deck furniture the week before, and the commode hadn't so much as a folding aluminum chair for company. The nearest object of note was thirty feet away—that gravestone.

For the rest of the day, I chuckled whenever I looked out the window. When our daughters came home from school, I told them to check out the deck. Same thing when my wife came home, and their reactions, in all three instances, were disappointing. When pressed, each admitted that, yes, out there the commode did look funny, in the sense of incongruous. Commodes, after all, are associated with small rooms; within those small rooms, they are often further enclosed. To see one sitting out in the open air, catching the last of the swirling autumn leaves, well, my wife and daughters conceded, they could understand why *someone* might find that amusing, maybe a man who's kind of weird to begin with. Nor, try as I might, could I make them understand why this commode/gravestone combo argued so compellingly against human pretension.

That said, I understood their position. A principal function of the adult human brain is to assign causes and classify observed phenomena. When we see something that strikes us as unusual, our instinct is to explain it in a way that makes it seem less so. Experience teaches us not to trouble ourselves unduly about the particular. Sure, we're encouraged to stop and smell the roses, but not all of them, not each one. That would take far too long, and the law of diminishing returns kicks in far too quickly. No, we take shortcuts that reinforce expectations. We learn to make leaps, because we'd lag behind if we didn't. When you walk into a house where men are laying tile in a bathroom and you see a commode sitting outside on a deck, the brain kicks into immediate overdrive, supplying a reason or cause. If it didn't, we would be overwhelmed with wonder at the magic of our existence, much as children are.

Part of a writer's job, of course, is to restore a little of that magic by slowing down the process by which these observations are organized and classified (and thus dispensed with), delaying explanations for what we're seeing at least long enough to enjoy, perhaps even marvel at, the thing itself. Explanations, in the final analysis, never satisfy us completely. They only reassure us, and that's a lesser achievement.

Okay, I admit it. I was sorry to see the commode return to its rightful place in our house, until I needed it to be there, after which I was grateful. A couple years later we ended up moving again. Robert Benton's wonderful film of *Nobody's Fool* came out and did well, introducing my work to a legion of readers who probably wouldn't have discovered it otherwise and convincing me that I could make it as a full-time writer. We bought a house on the coast of Maine in which I immediately claimed the biggest, brightest room for my office; my wife had been right to see this coming when I moved out of the Waterville house's cellar, and it's where I went to work on my novel *Empire Falls* while we waited for the old house to sell. For two years we waited, lowering the price, then again and yet again. It once came close to selling, until the would-be buyer flew his wife in and she saw the gravestone leaning up against that nasty apple tree. When our realtor called to give us the bad news, she said, "Could we lose that? The gravestone?" Because apparently there are things that sell houses—the aroma of fresh-baked muffins in the kitchen, for instance—and others, like gravestones, that send the wrong message. Anxious though we were to close the deal, we declined to move Nimon Kaleel Kater, who'd never done us or anyone else any harm that we knew of, and who'd been resting peacefully—or at least his stone had—in the shade of that tree for a good long while. Someone, I felt certain, would come along and appreciate poor Nimon, and eventually someone did.

Our reluctance to ditch that stone might suggest it played a more significant role in my writer's imagination than in fact it did. Though I'd been mowing around it for the past five years, I'd paid it very little actual attention. Guests would sometimes ask what it was doing there, and we'd explain that the house's first owner had been a stonecutter, and the conversation would move on.

It was the commode that somehow made the stone interesting. As a symbol, to that potential buyer's wife, the gravestone had been powerful enough to prevent a purchase, whereas I'd quickly noted its existence and then learned not to see it at all. The short life of Nimon Kaleel Kater, born in Syria at the turn of the century and dying in Waterville, Maine, of all places, twenty-eight years later, might have captured the imagination of many other writers, but not mine. I hadn't taken my daughters out to the apple tree and had them trace Nimon's name on the stone with their index fingers; I could have encouraged them to contemplate the mystery of this human life, once as real as their own, but I hadn't. Even as a symbol of my own mortality, the stone had failed to connect, whereas the commode had tickled my imagination ferociously, and this, I realized, could mean only one thing—that I am by temperament a comic writer, which means that's also my most natural way of looking at things; moreover, it's life's comedy I feel most compelled to share. This is important only because, as writers, many of our decisions about our work are predicated on impulse. Whether we even begin a story is often based on intuition. Will it be fruitful? we wonder, and often we proceed or not before reason is invited to participate in the discussion. The issue is self-knowledge, which is as necessary for a writer as for anyone else.

Most people agree that humor can't be taught. Someone already inclined toward a comic view of the world can sharpen that vision by working on timing and technique, and writers whose comedy runs out of control, diminishing their work's potential for seriousness, can learn restraint. But people who lack a sense of humor are unlikely to develop one through practice. They will remain like the narrator of *The Remains of the Day*, who wonders from time to time if he might learn to banter, though his forays into what he calls "witticism" are poor, sad affairs. Because humor looks easy, people want to know how it's done. My writing students used to ask, How do you make things so funny? To which I usually replied, I don't make anything funny. I'm simply reporting the world as I find it.

Some years ago I found myself in a Waffle House in Swannanoa, North Carolina, working on a lecture I was to deliver the next day at the MFA program at Warren Wilson College. It was midmorning and the place was empty except for me and the waitress who'd brought me my eggs and called me "hon," a sign of affection I much appreciated, especially after I'd asked if I might substitute hash browns for grits, revealing in this request that, yes, I was *from away*. A Yankee. It turned out she was on even more affectionate terms with the next fellow who strolled in and perched on a stool at the counter a few feet from my booth. "So how you doin', darlin'?" he said, after quickly taking my measure by the hash browns. "Jist fine," she replied, though she allowed, upon further questioning, that after finishing her shift she was heading to the dentist to have her lower front teeth pulled. She also had to decide what kind of a bridge she wanted—one the dentist cemented right there, permanent (unless somebody punched you in the mouth), or the sort you could remove at night and soak in a glass. She explained all this as the man ate his breakfast, and his interest wasn't feigned, because when she got to the part about teeth you could take out and soak, he wiped some yolk off his chin and said, "Yep, that's the kind I got," and promptly took out his uppers and offered them for her inspection. Seeing this surprising intimacy, I fully expected the woman to take at least one giant step back, as you would from *anybody* else's teeth, but of course we were in a Waffle House and I had her all wrong. Not the least squeamish, she took the man's choppers delicately between her thumb and forefinger and held them up to the bright, fluorescent light while he described the advantages and disadvantages, not all of which I could follow, since he clearly needed the teeth to make certain phonetic sounds. The waitress had no trouble following him, though, and by the time he finished, her mind was made up. She wanted teeth just like his, except pointing up, not down.

My point, naturally, is there's no need for any writer to make the world a funny place. It *is* a funny place, to anyone with eyes to see. Or, rather, with the right eyes. Because not everybody would truly *see* those teeth, or that commode on my back deck. A writer has to see things twice. First the thing itself, then its potential for a story. What he sees this second time is, in a sense, who he is. It's his artistic personality. What he doesn't see twice is just as revealing. I didn't truly see the gravestone's worth until it became part of a comic frame. That's when my initial interest was repaid, on this second viewing.

The problem for a writer with a genuinely comic imagination is not "making things funny" or even locating enough funny things in the real world to write about. Rather, the problem—and it's the same for any artist—is getting other people to see things as you do, to honor the truth of your idiosyncratic way of seeing. Art, in the end, may be little more than this: convincing people to set aside their natural reluctance long enough to register your vision. Isn't that what the impressionist painters ultimately succeeded in doing? The greatest obstacle comic writers face is that far more people truly see the gravestone than they do the commode. They look on the world and see death, ignorance, poverty, bigotry and injustice, and they see nothing funny in any of it. Worse, they suspect there must be something wrong with people who do. Such humorlessness does *not*—and I want to stress this—mean these people are stupid. Often they are among the kindest, most sensitive and generous people we know, which makes their blindness—for that's what it is—that much more difficult to deal with.

Some time ago I got into a heated argument at a dinner party with a woman I'll call Jane. We'd been friends for years, but she had no idea what she was stepping in when she remarked, innocently enough, "That's not funny." The subject was either speech impediments in general or stuttering in particular, I forget which, and in retrospect I realize there was probably no need for what ensued. Like so many unnecessary arguments, this one began by neither of us saying precisely what we meant, then defending the positions we'd clumsily staked out. We might very well have agreed, for instance, that it's not nice to make fun of people with speech impediments. I'm not nearly as nice a person as Jane, but I'm not inordinately cruel, either. Further, we might have agreed easily that stuttering isn't the least bit funny to the stutterer, especially if he or she is very young and self-conscious. Every day these people are betrayed by their bodies in ways that are difficult for the rest of us to imagine. This affliction makes them look foolish and slow-witted, and chances are they're neither.

But alas, my friend's position was that stuttering simply wasn't funny, and to this I took strident exception. For one thing, I thought I'd caught a whiff of righteousness in her pronouncement, and so was immediately on point. The example she used to illustrate her contention—the stammering actor in the movie *Shakespeare in Love,* who has such heroic difficulties introducing Will's play—was in my view far more useful to my point than to hers, and I said so. Of course I was more than casually invested here, since my novel *The Risk Pool* contains a stutterer (and years

later *Everybody's Fool* would feature another, even more promi-
nently). If I understood Jane's argument correctly, the screen-
writer of *Shakespeare in Love* was guilty not just of insensitivity by
abusing a fictional character, but also of causing unnecessary
pain to real-life stutterers who went to the movie and found
themselves the objects of mirth. If Jane was correct about the
moral landscape of the script, then by extension I owed an apology to my fictional character, as well as to any real-life stutterers who read the novel. The number of those cannot have been
large, because at the time not many people had, but still. I stood
accused.

"What about Michael Palin's character in *A Fish Called
Wanda?*" I said, mistakenly providing her with the very example she was at that moment trying to recollect in support of her
untenable position. "Are you seriously telling me," I asked, "that
Michael Palin trying to spit out 'Cathcart Hotel' to a frantically
impatient John Cleese isn't funny?" Indeed, my friend informed
me, it wasn't. Cruel is what it was, and she'd nearly walked out
of the theater. "Right," I mocked. "You n-n-nearly did." By now
Jane had withdrawn several layers deep, and her mouth was
clamped tightly shut in a thin line, but I didn't let up. "What
about the clergyman in *The Princess Bride?*" I forged ahead. I
could do a fair imitation of this character, and I leaned toward
Jane, not particularly bothered that she leaned away from me
as I said, "Wuv . . . twue wuv." There were a good half-dozen
people around the table, and except for Jane everyone was
laughing now. On a roll, I carried on about maybe the worst
real-life speech impediments I ever ran across. It belonged to
a good-natured fellow who used to take his large family to an
A&W Root Beer drive-in, where the kids invariably acted up.

The particular sound he had trouble forming was the letter *g*, which would come out like a *d* whenever he got excited. Naturally, the kids, who were all crammed into the backseat, liked to get out of the car and run around, slamming the doors and ignoring their father's instructions to cut it out, until he'd finally scream at them, much to the delight of people in nearby cars: "If you're donna dit in, dit in. If you're donna dit out, dit out. No more dod-damn dittin' in and dittin' out."

Well, it turned out this wasn't funny, either, according to Jane, which left me no choice but to parade every stutterer I knew, real and fictional, before the poor woman, who seethed in justifiable indignation at my boorish behavior. I didn't stop until I'd exhausted my entire store of speech-impediment memories, and then only reluctantly, finally allowing the conversation to move on, though, for the rest of the evening, whenever I saw natural color begin to return to Jane's cheeks, I leaned toward her and whispered, "Wuv . . . twue wuv." If she'd had a gun, I'm quite sure she'd have shot me dead, and to her way of thinking *that* would have been hilarious. Of course I called her the next morning and she graciously accepted my apology. "I guess humor is subjective," she allowed, making me wish I hadn't called. I hung up quickly when I felt the word "wuv" forming on my lips.

In the end, obviously, laughter is serious business, and the inability to laugh, at the world and at ourselves, is often, I believe, a sign of mental illness. In the weeks before her death, spiraling deeper and deeper into a depression she couldn't climb out of, Shirley Jackson wrote the same sentence over and over in her journal: *Laughter is possible.* In the throes of profound hopelessness, humor, its possibility, seemed like salvation, a rope dangling just beyond her grasp. Near the end of his own life Mark

Twain, overcome by loss and bitterness and despair, also stopped laughing, but he continued to believe in the power of laughter. The angel Satan in *The Mysterious Stranger* fragments, which were among the last things he ever wrote, reminds human beings that "against the assault of laughter, nothing can stand. You are always fussing and fighting with your other weapons. Do you ever use that one? No, you leave it rusting . . . you lack sense and courage." Or, as critic Katherine Powers puts it, "We Americans worry about humor, confusing it with a lack of seriousness. [But] look here. Along with art and immorality, it is humor that distinguishes human beings from animals. It is, furthermore, a truly civilizing force, nemesis to the big battalions, and a vexation and puzzlement to the purveyors of mediocrity."

To some it may seem counterintuitive that laughter should be a sign of high seriousness, but frequently it is. Laughter is often a more complex and thoughtful emotional response than tears, though we seem to believe that being moved to tears is somehow more noble. But surely Oscar Wilde was correct to ask who among us can read the death of Dickens's Little Nell in *The Old Curiosity Shop* without laughing, and mirth remains our best hedge against both sentimentality and self-importance, as well as a natural antidote to piety. Of course there are those who believe that needs no antidote. *Is nothing sacred?* they demand when their devotion is threatened. *Precious little* would be my reply, though we don't all draw the line in the same place. I didn't *want* the famous "Prom Night Dumpster Baby" sketch from *Family Guy* to be funny, because it was beyond tasteless. I was ashamed of myself for laughing at it. But don't tell me it's not funny. The test for funny is simple. Did you laugh? That we don't always feel good about ourselves afterward doesn't alter the fact.

Here's the thing: when people insist that something isn't funny, they're often expressing more of a wish than a conviction. For myriad reasons, we resist the complicity that humor demands. Feeling sympathy for stutterers, we would much prefer it if the affliction wasn't so comic. If we were better people, we suspect, it wouldn't be. We want to be better than we are and for the world to be a better, less cruel place than it is. Surely it *would* be a better place, such reasoning goes, if we could just suppress our own dubious natures. That our impulses are sinful, our natures fallen, is a puritan view, and this strain in American life has always run wide and deep.

I don't mean at all to suggest that everything is funny or that all things lend themselves equally well to humor. The September 11 attacks weren't funny, but it turns out that in the aftermath of the terrorism that brought down the World Trade Center, reports that irony was dead proved premature. Granted, the magnitude of the tragedy made it somewhere between difficult and impossible to imagine laughing again anytime soon. Like many writers, and not just comic ones, I felt for weeks, indeed months, that the act of filling an empty page with words was both futile and silly. But laugh we did, eventually, and that's nothing to be embarrassed by, never mind how uncomfortable those first laughs made us feel. Often such discomfort is the *purpose* of laughter, the point of the jest. Here's an ugly joke you've probably heard: What do you tell a woman with two black eyes? Answer: Nothing. She's already been told twice. Can such a joke be funny when domestic violence certainly is not? Well, that depends on a number of things, starting with whether you're a man or a woman. Also, whether you or someone you love has been a victim of violence. But beyond such personal considerations, there's also the question of whether you can accept and even embrace the contradictions that humor often demands. The absurd notion that for some men "telling" and "punching" are synonyms *is* amusing, at least in the abstract. Does the joke approve of such men and their behavior, or just acknowledge it and ask us to bear witness to its sad truth? The way some men laugh at this particular joke, their tone suggesting thorough appreciation, makes me, as a husband and father of two daughters, highly uncomfortable. *Yeah, that's the only way to tell a woman anything,* their amusement seems to imply. But at this point are we even talking about the joke itself, or has the focus moved on to the teller?

And that's another interesting subject. Haven't we all known people who somehow manage to get away with telling jokes that are tasteless, moronic and hurtful, while others get called out for jokes that are relatively benign? Context matters a great deal. In David France's book about the AIDS epidemic, *How to Survive a Plague,* he recalls a joke Bob Hope told at a fund-raiser. "The Statue of Liberty has AIDS," he informed his well-heeled audience, which included French president Mitterrand and his wife. "She got it either from the mouth of the Hudson or the Staten Island Ferry." To tell this joke at the height of the epidemic pushes defenders of both comedy and free speech pretty hard. Even *without* historical context it's right up there with "Prom Night Dumpster Baby" in terms of bad taste. At the same time, it's *in* context that the complexity of our reaction to humor often reveals itself. According to France, the Mitterrands were polite but clearly shocked and appalled. Nor did Nancy Reagan laugh, and given that she'd lost a dear friend—Rock Hudson—to AIDS earlier that year, it was probably impossible for her to separate the joke's merits (assuming it had any) from that painful context. Her husband, however, reportedly howled. Which begs an obvious question: Do we judge Mr. Reagan for laughing and, if so, according to what criteria? Aesthetically, the joke is hardly a knee-slapper. Is the president guilty of possessing an overly rudimentary sense of humor? Many people laugh at a volume of seven when the joke merits a two at most. What's the punishment for that? No, the real question is: Was his laughter *immoral*? Haven't we all been guilty of laughing at terribly inappropriate moments and felt the gut-wrenching complicity of having done so? If so, wouldn't it make sense to give Mr. Reagan (and, yeah, ourselves) a pass? Maybe. Until we recall, as France does, that Reagan didn't mention AIDS once during his first term in office and did everything in his power to withhold funding for AIDS research. And how about the cultural context of that laugh? Many in the United States, perhaps including Mr. Reagan himself, believed that AIDS was God's punishment on gays. But come on, you say. Aren't we making too much of all this? What's the matter, can't you take a joke? Well, whether you can or you can't often comes down to the perceived intention of the teller, and what's harder to pin down than intent? Hope was a professional comedian, so you might charitably conclude that his only intention was to make people laugh. Those who can get away with telling almost any joke manage that feat, I believe, by offering themselves, their totality, as proof they mean no harm. Personally, I refuse to give Bob Hope a pass because I'd long suspected he was a nasty piece of work, and the Statue of Liberty joke merely reinforced that suspicion. Much as I love a good laugh, I drew the line. I said, à la my friend Jane: *That's not funny.* Was I right? I've given it a lot of thought, and the truth is I don't know.

My decades-long friendship with the writer Jenny Boylan is based in large part on a shared vision of the world, which seems to us poised in Manichaean balance between hilarity and heartbreak. Our friendship has not only survived Jenny's transitioning from male to female but also, I believe, been strengthened by it. I can remember only one instance when we've had a serious disagreement and it was over a joke. In the afterword to her memoir *She's Not There* I recalled an incident where another transgender woman who, recovering from her surgery, had gotten an infection that caused a fever from which she might have died. I happened to discover this and reported her condition to her surgeon. On the phone the man seemed less concerned than baffled that such a thing could ever have occurred. Furious, I said, "Well, do you think it could have something to do with the fact that you cut her dick off?" Jenny practically begged me to delete that line from the piece, concerned that it made light of something serious, and even now I wouldn't argue that she was wrong. But at the risk of hurting one of my dearest friends, I stood my ground. The absurdity of the phrase *was* funny. More important, it went to the heart of the issue: you can't cut a woman's dick off because, by definition, she doesn't have one to begin with. Yet despite this compelling physical evidence, every transgender woman will tell you she *is* a woman. Her spirit—her soul, if you will—might be out of alignment with her body, but on whose authority should we conclude that physical reality trumps spiritual reality? Jenny, to her credit, accepted my decision not to cut the joke. Not because I'd convinced her. She didn't think I was right. What she accepted was *me*. I'd wounded her, but, knowing me, she knew that wasn't my intention.

And there's other reason laughter often makes us squirm:

it absolutely refuses to respect circumstance. It simply will not be confined or relegated, like dessert, to the end of the meal. It turns up, uninvited, at its own whim, seeming to enjoy our discomfort, even our humiliation. Before my father died of cancer, he willed his remains to medical science, joking that maybe the researchers could figure out what had made him tick, since he never could. As a result we weren't able to have a traditional funeral, which my father wouldn't have wanted anyway. I doubt he would've wanted the memorial service we held, either, but I did that much anyway. The notice in the paper, I thought, made all this abundantly clear.

The memorial was held at a large funeral home with several viewing rooms, though that afternoon my father's was the only service there. He had a lot of friends, and before long the place was crowded. We'd spilled out of the room we'd been assigned to into the hallway and adjacent rooms. I was not in the best of shape. Our relationship had been checkered, but in his final years we'd become close, and his loss hit me hard. I was working on *The Risk Pool,* a novel that was, though I didn't realize it then, a kind of valentine, a book that allowed my father and me to have the kind of conversation we were unlikely ever to have in real life. Here, I got to play both parts, a duty I accepted cheerfully enough until I learned he was ill, which meant that after he died I'd have to play both parts forever, a job I wasn't sure I was up to.

Everyone at the funeral home seemed to have a story to tell about my father, and I wasn't able to pay much attention to anyone except whomever I happened to be speaking to at the moment, but at the periphery of my consciousness I became aware of a wizened old man who'd entered the funeral home uncertainly and begun to look around, as if for a daughter or son he hoped to lean on. Weaving unsteadily among the crowd, squeezing in between taller people, he methodically made his way down the hall and into the viewing room, where the majority of visitors were congregated. Five minutes later he emerged, seemingly still on a mission, crossing the hallway into the second viewing room, then minutes later into the third. Not long after this I saw him heading up the stairs into what were surely the private living quarters of the people who ran the home. There, midinvestigation, he must have been discovered, because when he reappeared on the stairs, he was guided by a woman I took to be the funeral director's wife. She had the old fellow firmly by the elbow, clearly determined to return him downstairs, but at the landing he stopped, refusing to budge until he'd received some satisfaction. No doubt he understood that on the floor level, he'd never be able to attract anyone's attention, whereas here he had the required loft. "Ahem!" he said, his voice surprisingly strong. Most everyone looked up. "Where the hell is Jimmy?" was what he wanted to know.

When I say that laughter is often a more complex and thoughtful emotion than tears, *this* is what I mean. And when the old man posed this question, I laughed out loud, in spite of myself. That laugh contained, among other things, a small release from the pain of loss and an understanding of the old man's frustration; he'd never been to a memorial service before and had no idea what it was. There was also guilt, the result of laughing during a solemn occasion, as well as a grim acknowledgment that the old man's question echoed my own, for all day long I'd been imagining my father, his cancer-wasted body lying out on some slab, under the scalpel of a physician motivated purely by scientific curiosity. Indeed, where the hell *was* my father? The final test of what's funny or not is whether it's true. Of course I don't mean if some incident actually happened, or even if the story has been embellished or exaggerated. What I mean is: Is it true to our experience of life? Is this the way people really are? Is this how the world truly works? Not coincidentally, this is the test of all good writing, not just comic writing.

The best humor has always resided in the chamber next to the one occupied by suffering. There's a door adjoining these rooms that's never completely closed. Sometimes it's open just a crack, because that's all we can stand. Most of the time it's flung wide open on a well-oiled hinge, and this is as it should be. Those in favor of shutting it tight are always, *always* wrong. The gravestone and the commode coexist in this world, and it's our job neither to ignore nor segregate them, no matter how attractive the separation is made by grief and loss. In John Bayley's eloquent memoir *Elegy for Iris,* he describes, in heartbreaking detail, the descent of his beloved wife into Alzheimer's. Near the end, novelist Iris Murdoch would remember almost nothing about her life, her work or any of the things that had meant the most to her, including the man who was now taking care of her. What she did recall, longer than just about anything else, Bayley says, were the punch lines to jokes she and her husband had always loved. The context of these had fled, sadly, and the poor woman would have been hard-pressed to remember any of the jokes' elements, but all Bayley had to do was to say a punch line and Iris would laugh, remembering that, whatever he'd just said, it had once been funny. Bayley concludes from this—and I think he's right—that nothing is more fundamental to our shared humanity than laughter. Unless, of course, it's wuv. Twue wuv.

Getting Good

Almost the whole capital of the novelist is the slow accumulation of unconscious observation.

—Mark Twain

I was in junior high—as middle school was called back then—when I heard my first live band. The venue was the same gym where we hormone-driven eighth-grade boys ran laps, climbed ropes, played dodgeball and wrestled, in the process converting our recent cafeteria lunch—half a ham-salad sandwich and a shallow bowl of Campbell's tomato soup—to methane. I'd been to dances before at the YWCA, but in that smaller gym a DJ spun records. This was different. Hearing the same songs I'd listened to on the radio thundering through guitar amplifiers, the insistent bass thumping so hard that the bleachers vibrated, was a revelation. I all but levitated. This was for me.

The boys in the band were older by what—two or three years? Four at the most, but an eternity back then. And cool? Dear God. Their longish, shiny hair was slicked back on the sides, their pompadours somehow dangling down over their foreheads and swaying to the music's urgent beat. They wore white shirts and narrow ties, dark jackets and tight "pegged" pants. When they stepped up to the microphone to sing "Baby, Wha'd I Say," they seemed almost to whisper into the mics, but their voices boomed and echoed off the walls, pulses and crackles of their low-slung Fender guitars seeming disconnected from both the fingers of their left hands, which flew over the frets, and their barely moving right hands, as they picked and strummed. The songs themselves weren't "perfect," like the more polished and heavily orchestrated versions played on the radio, but to me they were *so* much better. Hearing the former, you'd smile and nod your head. In the gym—never mind the wafting aroma of dirty socks and sour jockstraps—you could sense in every ringing, echoing note the thrilling proximity of something you couldn't name or even describe. Freedom was part of it, but, more than that, power. Music played this loud by tall, lean boys showed even the school's thick-necked bullies what mattered and what didn't. Though trying to look nonchalant, they hung on every note as hungrily as dweebs like me. The boys behind those roaring sunburst guitars altered our world and in the same instant ruled it. It would be decades before I'd want anything as much as I did to be one of them. Before that eighth-grade moment my most fervent wish had been that my father, long banished, might return to the house my mother and I shared with my grandparents in an upstate New York mill town. Afterward, there were things I needed more than him and an intact family. A guitar. An amp. A mic.

What do you *do* with such visceral yearning?

If all you have is a cheap acoustic guitar, you start saving the money from your after-school job for a cheap electric one, and after that you somehow manage to buy a secondhand amplifier about a quarter of the size of those in the gym. Everything that comes out of it sounds fuzzy because some other boy with a need identical to yours has blown one of its two tiny speakers. Next, you join forces with a kid who dreams of being a drummer and whose parents have promised him a set for Christmas, and another boy who also plays guitar—his is better than yours—and has a decent amp. When the drummer gets his drums, his parents let you practice in their basement. Somehow, somewhere, you locate a couple microphones, which means both mics and guitars are now plugged into your good amp. It takes you forever to find the setting that doesn't result in earsplitting feedback. Your drummer doesn't think of the band as a collaboration so much as a competition between members. He wants to bang, so bang he does. The song he's beating out is only tangentially related to the one the guitars are playing. He works himself into a frenzy of wallops that don't take into consideration where you are in the song, its slow build toward climax. Sometimes he doesn't even notice when you stop playing, just keeps pounding until he's spent. He hates ballads because he's not permitted to work himself into his preferred ecstatic state.

You suck, but you keep practicing. The drummer takes lessons, improves. You all do, though it's hard to tell how much because your needs—better instruments, amps and mics—are so great, so far beyond your economic reach. Also, you need an audience. You need feedback and not the sort that comes out of your amplifier when you turn up the guitars and the mics so you can be heard over the drums. One of the few things you need that doesn't cost money is a name for the band, so you obsess about that as if it were your most pressing concern. You go through the list of car names, most of which have been taken. Have you arrived on the scene too late? You need to look like a band, which means clothes. You can't afford the skinny black suits those other boys had, and even if you could your parents would never let you out of the house looking like that. They understand you're in the grip of something powerful, though, so they confer and buy you matching fuzzy sweaters, powder blue.

Even though it costs money to enter, you sign up for a county-wide Battle of the Bands to be waged at the old armory, where three or four hundred kids will hear you. Even as you set up your equipment, long before the first note is struck, you can tell the other four bands will be better. With your two small amps you won't be heard above the ambient noise of the crowd, and the tiny part of you that's tethered to reality whispers in your ear that this may be a blessing in disguise. You're up first. People are still arriving when you play your two-song set, which only people standing next to you can hear. Later your friends drift over and ask when you're going on, and you have to explain that you already did. No surprise, you finish last. Fifth out of five. Nor, as it turns out, is this the worst humiliation of the evening. In the armory parking lot, you watch the boys in the other bands load their instruments into an armada of vehicles—pickup trucks, vans, rented U-Haul trailers; the winning band has a repurposed hearse. Yours is the only band whose equipment fits, with room to spare, into one rig, the back of the drummer's parents' pathetically uncool Nash Rambler station wagon.

Monday, after school, you do a postmortem. You tell yourself you'd sound better with better equipment, but in your heart of hearts you know you'd only sound louder. At the end of the week, your other guitarist announces he's quitting and taking with him the only good amp. Face it, you're a joke. You and the drummer, sick at heart, look for another guitarist. You hear about a Jewish kid who's supposed to be good, so you give him a try, and he *is* good. He's been studying classical guitar for several years and seems not even to have heard of rock and roll. You invite him to join the band anyway because there's nobody else. You tell him where his parents can buy the requisite powder-blue sweater.

Since you're fourteen, you don't understand that far worse than not *having* what you need is not *knowing* what you need. That you need so much—better instruments, a sound system that's separate from your guitar amplifier, the means to get to gigs in the unlikely event that anyone hires you—obscures the fact that what you need most, which renders your other needs irrelevant, is to get good. Right now all you've really got is this terrible, relentless hunger to strap on a Fender Stratocaster, plug it into a killer amp, step up to the mic and make the kind of music that doubles as a sledgehammer. Nothing else matters.

Hunger has no business preceding ability, but it always does, with no exceptions.

If my maternal grandfather were alive today, I'd ask him whether he considered himself an artist. I'm pretty sure he'd say no, that he was just a glove cutter. That was how he made his living, and he was good at it. He *got* good by joining a guild, apprenticing himself to craftsmen who knew what they were doing. If memory serves, this period lasted for two years, during which he learned the skills that could be taught and carefully observed his mentors—not just the tricks of their trade but their demeanor—in the hopes of intuiting what couldn't be. I don't know how much people in this position made back then, but according to my aunt he was largely dependent on the generosity of whoever he was working with. He couldn't afford to marry my grandmother until he finished his apprenticeship, though, so it's safe to say he wasn't overpaid. Indeed, during his entire career as a glove cutter he would never be overpaid. By the time he entered it, the leather industry had already fallen victim to disruption and was, at least in America, circling the drain. When he was young and new to his trade, being good still mattered, so getting good was the first imperative. By the time he retired, being good mattered only to him.

The principal tools of a guild-trained glove cutter were a good pair of shears and his imagination. He didn't need to be told how big a size 6 pair of ladies' gloves were. That knowledge was in his hands, and the shears he was holding were an extension of those hands. Imagination was required, because each skin was riddled with blemishes that could be minimized but not eliminated. The trick, my grandfather explained to me as a boy, was to maneuver the skin in such a way that its imperfections would be hidden in the stitching and the narrow fingers, and kept out of plain view in the broad palm and the long stretch of wrist and forearm. A lesser craftsman wouldn't worry about these subtleties; he just got as many gloves as possible out of the skin. But to men like my grandfather, each skin was a puzzle. You studied it for a good long while, mulling over its challenges, planning your strategy to diminish their impact, before you ever picked up your shears.

Not every craft rises to the level of art, at least not in the traditional sense, but arts and crafts are often linked and for good reason. Speed is the enemy of both, and neither can abide carelessness. Central to both enterprises is a species of optimism, a faith that the task is feasible and worth accomplishing. Both require a plan, as well as the wisdom to abandon that plan should doing so become necessary. The director Fred Schepisi tells a story about the time he invited an oral surgeon to his film class. Dimming the lights, the man tacked to the wall a group of backlit X-rays, different shots of the same mouth, which anyone could see, even in these ghostly representations, was a complete clusterfuck. Some teeth needed to be pulled, some rotated, others pushed back or forward or sideways. Nor could everything be done at once. Proper sequencing was essential. *B* had to follow *A*, because it was going to cause *C*, which would determine whether you needed to address *D* or could skip right to *E*. It took the oral surgeon the full class period to map out his complex strategy for rectifying nature's botched job.

When the lights came up, one of Fred's puzzled students asked the obvious question: What did dentistry have to do with making movies? "More than you'd think," Fred told him. Most complex human endeavors, he explained, require skill and intelligence, and talent always helps, but in addition to these you'll also need intuition—the ability to recognize what's related to what, as well as what at first glance appears related but actually isn't. Your strategy should be flexible enough to take into account not just the difficulties you've anticipated but also those you haven't, because things *will* go wrong. In every movie you'll make at least one costly casting mistake. And then there's serendipity. On the day you most need the sun to come out, it won't, or if it does, it'll go behind the only cloud in the sky at precisely the wrong moment, ruining your most important shot. The actor you've got for only three weeks—who's committed to four other films after yours—will break his foot stepping out of the limo. You think this guy's *mouth* is a clusterfuck? Just you wait.

Indeed, a good hint that you've entered the realm of Art is that you immediately feel like giving up. You become overwhelmed by the astonishing complexity of the task, the sheer number of moving parts over which you have less-than-perfect control, the perversity of happenstance, the impossibility of predicting outcomes. In *Life on the Mississippi* Twain describes learning to pilot a steamboat as an art because the river you steam up this week isn't the same one you'll navigate after a week of rains on your return trip. It's still the Mississippi and eventually you'll end up in New Orleans, not some unexpected city, but each trip is different because the river is. You have to know everything about it, know it without having to think, and be certain of your judgments, which will have to be made quickly on the basis of incomplete information, and at night you'll have to do all this and more by feel. It would be nice if the river were a science because in the sciences there are controls, and if you've been careful your results can be replicated. What worked on Tuesday will work on Thursday, a claim that cannot always be made when what you hold in your hand is a paintbrush or a camera or a pen. What was exactly right for your last painting will be completely wrong for this one. Creative people love to claim they know what *works*, but in reality all they know is what *worked*. Fortunes are lost and hearts broken in that shift of tense.

As I say, I don't know if my grandfather thought of himself as an artist, but I'm convinced that in explaining his craft he was giving me my first valuable lesson in art, and I've remembered it often when contemplating the flaws in whatever narrative I happened to be working on, as well as any defects (at least the ones I'm aware of) in my own character, those gifts that keep on giving.

What little I know about the guild my grandfather joined as a young man suggests that it had more in common with the Renaissance guilds of northern Europe than modern unions. If you wanted to be a painter in Delft, you would apprentice to a master for pretty much the same reason my grandfather did in upstate New York three centuries later: you wanted to get good. There were two basic requirements to join: you had to come up with a fee, and you had to demonstrate an aptitude. At the end of your apprenticeship, if you couldn't cut it, you were out. No recourse. A guild jury said no, and that was it for you. Were you allowed to paint or sculpt outside its auspices? Sure, if you could afford canvas and paint and clay. That is, you were allowed to have a hobby. You just couldn't get hired.

Was the system just? I doubt it. Given how tough it's always been for artists to make ends meet, I have to assume the guild system that produced Vermeer and Rembrandt must've been brutally competitive, and in any system there are injustices. There must've been talented men who couldn't afford the fee, rendering their talent moot. And what if a man (and we *are* talking about men here, both in seventeenth-century Delft and in Gloversville, New York, circa 1920) came up with the necessary fee and then, early on, showed no talent, or not enough? Was there some slow-learner version of Rembrandt cut adrift before he could flower? It happens. In graduate school I watched more than one apprentice writer make the same mistakes story after story, seemingly unable to grasp what was going wrong, until one day, sometimes years later, the light would come on, and the work would take a quantum leap forward. That doesn't do you much good if you've already been judged and found wanting.

What was the mission of the Renaissance guilds? You might imagine it would be the protection of its members, and you'd be partly right. There's always been both safety and power in numbers, and guild members undoubtedly benefited from their association. But the guild's mission was also to protect and defend Art itself, to prevent it from being cheapened. The relationship of guildsmen to their craft was proprietary. Put differently, they had little use for hacks. They didn't hate them, or publicly ridicule them, or burn them at the stake. But they would've been horrified by the kind of egalitarianism that Maria Semple skewers in her satirical novel *Where'd You Go, Bernadette?*: "Everyone is equal. Joni Mitchell is interchangeable with the secretary at open mic night . . . John Candy is no funnier than Uncle Lou when he gets a couple beers in him." Central to the mind-set of the Renaissance guildsman was the responsibility of making value judgments. Not everything is art. Not everyone is talented. Therefore, not everyone can join.

Of course some modern unions are also notoriously difficult to join. The reason, though, usually has less to do with art than with commerce. Higher-wage union jobs are (or used to be) much sought after, and because union workers can be hard to fire, so membership becomes a kind of sinecure. Many of the union guys I've worked with over the years took great pride in being good at what they did, and when I was growing up there was a general perception that a union plumber, carpenter or electrician was probably a cut above his nonunion competition. But modern unions came into being to keep workers from being exploited, to make certain that workplaces were safe, that workers—many of them unskilled, uneducated and therefore easily taken advantage of—made a living wage and that the lion's share of the profits didn't disappear into the employers' pockets. While it may be true that most workers would prefer to do good work to shoddy work, a union's primary mission isn't to guarantee quality but rather to ensure its members are treated fairly. Unlike guilds, unions negotiate contracts and make certain they're honored. The equation is economic, not proprietary, at least not in the Renaissance sense. Union electricians don't worry inordinately about the integrity, health and overall well-being of electricity.

I'm certain my grandfather understood this distinction and felt the ideological conflict. A guild man, he nevertheless helped his fellow glove cutters, many of them unskilled and marginally literate, to unionize. Tanneries and glove shops were dangerous places, and before workers organized, their wages were depressed, their safety concerns largely ignored. The union helped, though its victories, at least according to my grandfather, were pretty modest. Its members were, to use one of my old man's favorite expressions, shoveling shit against the tide. Every year more and more jobs went overseas, where labor was cheap and the industry unregulated. Both the guys who worked in the glove shops and the women who sewed gloves at home understood all too well that the weak hand they'd been dealt was only getting weaker. Many placed their faith in the disruptive new technology that was undermining their craft. Pattern cutting—where a size-6 paper pattern was affixed to the skin and cut around, and then the skin was stitched up—became the industry norm. Later, even this time-consuming labor was dispensed with. "Clicker-cutting" machines capable of stamping out one pair of size-6 ladies' gloves after another, as fast as the skin could be stretched beneath those lethal blades, were invented, and any dimwit could pull those levers. Chromium, though lethal, sped up the tanning process. Piecework did the rest. Men anxious to make as much money as possible disabled safety mechanisms while the foremen looked the other way. Speed was officially king, rendering craft irrelevant. Suddenly, throughout the entire ecosystem, nobody seemed to give a shit. Shop owners made it clear that they wanted as many gloves as possible out of each skin, blemishes be damned. Technology was pushing prices down, which made consumers happy. Who cared if the merchandise was shoddy?

Well, my grandfather did, which probably explains why he never prospered in the new system. Used to being held to a higher standard, he never got the hang of the lower one. He must've known it would be more advantageous not to care, but he didn't have it in him. Seeing what was coming at him and recognizing it as the future, he just couldn't escape. He was like the Mississippi riverboat captains Twain idolized in *Life on the Mississippi*. They too had been represented by a guild, a powerful one; it disappeared when they did, almost overnight.

Me? I'm both a guild man, like my grandfather, and a union man, like my father. At the time of this writing I'm vice president of the Authors Guild, an organization dedicated to defending the writing life, which in our view is endangered thanks to the digital disruption, the continued erosion of copyright protection, Amazon's relentless drive toward monopoly status as the nation's bookseller, the low price of e-books that's threatening the economic model of print books, the refusal of traditional publishers to share the wealth they're reaping from digital publication and continued pressure on the physical bookstores that have always been our showrooms and have helped make possible the careers of writers like me.

I'm also a member of the Writers Guild, an association of screenwriters who work in film and television and, increasingly, for the web. This guild is really a union. Its members bargain collectively. When negotiations break down, they go on strike and the film industry grinds to a very public halt. The rules for membership couldn't be more elegant. You can't join unless you have a writing deal, but once you get one you can't *not* join. You don't have to be a good writer; someone just has to hire you. The guild has a minimum contract that ensures all members are decently compensated, though naturally the more success-ful screenwriters make more. A lot more. If your first script is a box-office sensation or earns you an award nomination, you can go straight to the head of the salary line. People who have been guild members for forty years might be in the back, but the minimum contract provides them with a living wage, medical coverage and a pension plan.

By contrast, the writers who make up the Authors Guild don't bargain collectively, don't go on strike, don't shut publishing houses down when we can't come to terms. There is no mini-mum contract that publishers must abide by, nor could there be. Small publishers often pay far less than a living wage, and some large publishers don't pay much more for the work of midlist authors. While most Writers Guild members make their liv-ing writing scripts, members of the Authors Guild increasingly require some other means of support to make ends meet. Many teach or have other full- or part-time jobs. As individual contractors, they don't get health insurance, nor do their publishers set money aside for their pension plans. The AG does have a dedicated legal department that will go over contracts and point out where publishers' contracts are predatory or outside established norms, but it has neither the authority nor leverage to insist on better terms. What power the guild possesses derives not just from our numbers but from the fact that many of its members are household names. Screenwriters, with notable exceptions, are not nearly so famous. The scripts they write may be the foundation of great movies, but most of the fame and glory goes to actors and directors. Where membership in the Writers Guild is clear-cut—you can't belong until you have to—in the Authors Guild it's murkier. When you publish your first book with a trade publisher, you'll likely get a letter from the AG inviting you to join, but you aren't required to, nor are you badgered if you decline. You don't have to make a lot of money to join, but you do have to earn some to demonstrate that you're a professional, not a hobbyist.

The primary difference between these two guilds and the one my grandfather joined in upstate New York or that Johannes Vermeer joined in Delft is that you don't have to provide evidence of talent. Indeed, you can demonstrate the opposite, book after book, script after script. The stated mission of the Authors Guild—to defend the writing life—is, I believe, worthwhile, but it's not nearly so high-minded as the mission of the Renaissance guilds. The latter probably would have scoffed at the notion that you could protect an artist's life if you disavowed responsibility to the art that made that life possible. Outsourcing the organization's primary moral duty would've been unthinkable. Suffice it to say, the medieval/Renaissance worldview no longer has relevance.

That's not to say that nobody cares about quality anymore. Who decides what's good these days? Who's an artist and who's a hack? Well, publishers, agents, MFA programs, retreats like Yaddo and MacDowell, the National Endowment for the Arts, the Guggenheim and MacArthur Foundations, innumerable juried prizes, professional newspaper, radio and TV reviewers, bloggers and the opinionated staffs of independent bookstores, to name just a few. These are the cultural gatekeepers, and there seem to be more of them now than ever before, probably because there are more gates.

Not everyone agrees that all these gatekeepers serve a useful purpose. Some writers, particularly those working in various genres, have done well publishing their own books. To judge by their output, many are extremely hardworking, putting out three or four new titles a year, and the jury they care most about is the individual reader who's thinking about clicking the BUY button. Many of these indie authors have no particular fondness for brick-and-mortar bookstores because these don't contribute significantly, or maybe at all, to their bottom line. Physical books? If you don't sell many print books, or any, you probably don't care much if these disappear. Not surprisingly, writers whose incomes derive chiefly from online sales embrace technologies—e-books, self-publishing platforms, the Internet itself—that have so disrupted the publishing industry and, in their view, leveled the playing field. Many self-published authors pride themselves on what they've learned to do without: agents, marketing folks, publicists, editors and in some cases, alarmingly, even copy editors—that army of sycophants who (again, in their view) siphon off an unfair share of the income from the author's labor and in the process erect unnecessary barriers between writer and reader, which, to hear them tell it, is the only truly necessary relationship in publishing. Despite charging as little as $1.99 per e-book (and sometimes less), some indies claim to be making a ton of money because they're able to keep up to 70 percent of the book's price, compared with the miserly 10 to 15 percent offered by traditional publishers on expensive hardcovers and generally just 7.5% on paperbacks. Some indies are even willing to give their books away for short periods of time, believing that such largesse will boost sales in the long term. Hearing them argue so convincingly for how little their work is worth, even to them, may strike some as sad, but that's not how they see it, and they have their reasons. Before self-publishing, they had nothing and no recourse. Now they have careers (yes, modest ones, some admit, but that's also increasingly true of midlist authors with traditional publishers). More important, they have hope. Their self-reliance is positively Emersonian, and they love being at the controls.

Their most beguiling argument for getting rid of the gatekeepers, however, isn't economic but political and moral. Many writers who have been rejected or haven't prospered with mainstream publishers argue in language reminiscent of the current national debate over income inequality: like America's poor, they feel the deck is stacked against them. Moreover, the converse is also true: those who *have* prospered with traditional publishers aren't better writers, just privileged ones. They've gone to the right schools, had access to the sort of people who can make the necessary introductions. Arriving at the door of the gatekeepers' club, they already know the secret handshake. E-books and self-publishing offer a not-so-fond farewell to all that. Thanks to disruptive technology, you no longer need an expensive education, or family wealth, or an introduction, and you certainly don't have to join any guild. Instead you have your own sweet voice, connected to your own agile intellect. And on the day when mainstream publishing goes the way of Mississippi riverboat captains, when all their attendant gatekeepers are shown the door, those of us who benefited from their good opinion won't know what hit us. On that day of reckoning—yeah, they sound a lot like fundamentalist Christians awaiting the rapture—there will be no more artists and no more hacks, just writers, just you and your Amazon ranking and readers, their index fingers poised over the I-CLICK button. *Then* we'll see how writers used to lavish advertising budgets and publicist-driven review attention will do when they have to slug it out in the trenches.

This faux-democratic argument is bolstered when the gatekeepers get it spectacularly wrong, which does happen. The book that's been rejected by every major publishing house goes on to become a runaway digital bestseller and a movie with an A-list star, after which its author is belatedly signed to a lucrative three-book deal. It's a deeply satisfying narrative, and some variation on this theme exists across the entire spectrum of the arts. The painter, sculptor, poet or musician who's worked in obscurity her whole life is suddenly discovered and proclaimed a major artist. Who doesn't like stories about people who aren't supposed to win but manage to anyway? Much of the satisfaction derives from the fact that the so-called experts are proven to be clueless. Everyone who's ever been told they aren't good enough gets a new lease on life, and let's face it: that's most people.

Revolutionary zeal and rhetoric aside, however, this longed-for outcome doesn't seem terribly likely. Sure, people enjoy wandering around art fairs, looking for bargains and undiscovered talent, but they also rely on curators. Even people who know how to think and reserve the right to come to their own conclusions like to hear professional opinions. Satisfying though it may be when the gatekeepers get it wrong, people appreciate juried shows. Anyone who has doubts on this score need only stand in line at the Louvre or the Guggenheim when a new show opens. The more information there is in the world, the greater our need for curators to arrange and make sense of it. Okay, expert witnesses can be bought, but so can Amazon reviews. If the pros aren't always unbiased, neither are Yelp reviewers. Thanks to my father, I can read a racing form and find most of the data I need, but I don't go to the track every day, and there are people who do. Before I plunk down my two bucks, I'm curious to know what they think. Though I might not follow their advice, I do want to hear it, because not all opinions are of equal value. And even if you *could* toss out one gaggle of tastemakers, another would arise to replace it. We value insight. John Candy *was* funnier than Uncle Lou when he had a couple beers in him. If Uncle Lou could've been John Candy, he would've been.

My daughter Kate is a painter. Growing up, she felt fundamentally different from her older sister, Emily (who's now an independent bookseller), as well as her parents, all of us being voracious readers. Coming into a room and finding the three of us immersed in a book, she wanted to scream. She tried to love words like we did, but it just wasn't happening. More to the point, words didn't love her. They had a habit of rearranging themselves on the page, mocking her. Only when there was an accompanying chart or graph or illustration did their meaning become clear. In short, she was a visual learner. Highly intuitive, she was forever mystifying us with bizarre comparisons between how something sounded and how something else tasted. "There you go again, dancing about architecture," I'd tease, though in fact I was intrigued by how her mind worked. Art is often about making connections that other people don't notice. In college Kate majored in studio art and art history, then got an MFA at the Slade School in London, where she met her husband, who's also an artist.

It's been a joy and a privilege to watch them pursue their careers, but painful too, because it takes a long time to get really good and because getting good is no guarantee of success. I know from experience that when success doesn't come, especially after a large expenditure of time and faith and, yes, money, the little voice that whispers to you about now being an excellent time to give up gains traction and begins to sound like the voice of reason. Sometimes it *is* the voice of reason, because not a few aspiring artists delude themselves, choosing to believe that their small talent is a large one, or by telling themselves that they've come too far to quit when acclaim is surely right around the corner. Popular culture teaches us that those who fail didn't want success badly enough, as if hunger and faith were the best predictors of it. In reality, hunger and faith, absent talent, or at least a certain facility, is more often a prescription for heartbreak. Music was the great love of my maternal grandmother's life, but to hear her sing was to glimpse God's sometimes-cruel sense of humor. It took a lifetime of people covering their ears to convince her that what she was hearing when she sang had little to do with the sound she was actually making. Ironically if your talent *is* mediocre, you're much worse off, because your need will make a Calvinist of you. You'll be constantly on the lookout for signs that you are among the elect, or at least not (like my grandmother) among the damned. You'll try as best you can to compare your native talent with that of other artists, even if you understand that native talent is yet another piss-poor predictor of "election." Or you'll try to compare your effort and hunger and need with theirs, though of course the last two are unknowable, unquantifiable and possibly irrelevant to boot. Every day you ask yourself whether to soldier on or cut your losses and start making some money, like your friends are doing. Or maybe take a job in a related field so as to remain close to your object of desire, however much you suspect that proximity is no substitute for the intimacy you crave.

Back in high school, Kate was the friend of a talented kid a couple years older, who also wanted to be a painter. At the time we were living in a Maine mill town that was home to an expensive liberal arts college where I was teaching. Predictably, the town's public schools cleaved along class lines, kids whose parents worked in the mills on one side, the children of professors and administrators on the other. Kate's friend was also a faculty brat, but in his senior year he fell in with a bunch of would-be artists, many of them older, who imagined themselves contemporary Kerouacs and Pollocks and Ginsbergs. They rented a rancid loft downtown, dressed in black, drank, smoked a lot of dope and worked on their sneers. Being young and serious and rebellious, Kate's friend was much impressed, and before long he was talking their party line. There was no point in going to college, he insisted, or in studying with the kind of artists who taught there (like his parents, like me), just failures and sellouts, most of them. There were painters long before there were MFAs in painting, he argued, and you certainly didn't need a fancy gallery to sell a picture. Screw the tastemakers and gatekeepers. All you really needed were brushes and paint and canvas and a place to work. The rest was bullshit. The only important relationship was the one between the artist and the viewer. In a perfect (highly implausible) world everything would be free.

There is, of course, just enough truth in all of the above to make it seductive, and what's patently false is the most seductive because it plays to democratic impulses. It troubled Kate that her friend, who was in fact talented, should have come to such conclusions. When he became strident—"No one can teach me anything," he told her proudly, without visible irony—and contemptuous of anyone who disagreed, he was impossible to like, which was why, for a time, they fell out of touch. My wife and I felt bad about this, and not only because we were friends with his parents. The following year, at their insistence, he went off to college, then dropped out after his freshman year and moved to New York City, where he was rumored to be living in extreme poverty and hanging out with a dicey crowd. Years later I saw him, a young man now, selling his paintings one day on West Broadway in Lower Manhattan. I thought about going over and saying hello, and I should have, but I wasn't sure he'd be happy to see someone he used to disapprove of. He would likely inquire after Kate, and I'd certainly tell him she'd just graduated from the Slade in London, where she'd won a competitive drawing prize. He'd probably take my fatherly pride as proof that I didn't consider him a real artist who'd be showing in a gallery, not on West Broadway or in Washington Square. I feared, in other words, he would take me for the snob that I probably was at that moment, because what did I really know about him after so many years? He'd been a great kid, a guest in our house and a friend of my daughter, and I hadn't even gone around to the right side of the easel to look at his work.

Self-published writers are often treated with this same disdain. They get tired of being told that their work must be dreck because it hadn't found a traditional publisher. And who can blame them for resenting those who conclude without reading their work that they must be talentless hacks because of how they've chosen to publish? By the same logic you'd belittle the gifted minor-league ballplayer who just isn't ready for the majors. Are indie authors wrong to resent that self-published books are seldom reviewed, often not eligible for prizes or awards, and they're not invited to join many professional associations (excepting the Authors Guild). If they publish with Amazon, most independent bookstores—understanding that Amazon, like Barnes & Noble and Borders before it, is trying to put them out of business—won't stock their print-on-demand physical books.

A couple years after I saw him on West Broadway, I heard that Kate's old high-school friend was actually doing quite well. He not only was regularly selling his paintings but also had several commissions. Another friend reported that he was making serious money. And every day, it seems, another midlist author with bad sales numbers is dropped by his publisher or, feeling abandoned, decides he or she has nothing to lose by self-publishing. Lonely paths, either one.

———

I joined my first union—the Laborers'—in 1967. That allowed me to work road construction with my father, who'd been a member himself only for a few years. I don't recall how much it cost to join, which probably means my father paid for it, just as he paid my dues all year long so there'd be a job waiting for me when I returned from college. Most years I earned enough during those summer months to cover my tuition and fees at the University of Arizona, which says something about both the union wage and the bargain higher education was back then, especially at large state universities in the West. I still remember what I made that first summer: $3.33 an hour, a breathtaking sum compared with what men like my grandfather were making in the skin mills. Think about that. An unskilled eighteen-year-old making more per hour than a sixty-year-old craftsman?

In movies and on TV, the union-employer relationship is usually depicted as adversarial and contentious, which it often is, but when I remember those summers working with my father, I'm amazed at how often they saw eye to eye. Back then (and maybe now, for all I know) the pay on most construction jobs was pretty egalitarian. My first summer I worked on a grading crew, mindless, backbreaking work that didn't require an ounce of talent or intelligence. Carpenters, plumbers, electricians and other skilled workers made more than laborers, of course, their contracts negotiated by their own unions. And if you were a foreman, you made more than the rest of your crew. Otherwise you didn't get much credit for rank or how hard, according to your foreman, you worked. I made the same hourly wage as my father, though he knew what he was doing and I didn't. With his lean, tough, scrap-iron body, he could do more work in three hours than I, soft from nine months of sitting in the university library, could do in eight, at least until midsummer when I rounded into shape. The construction companies that hired us college boys had to know they weren't getting their money's worth, especially when bad weather put them behind schedule and we all went on overtime. We weren't treated like today's interns, expected to work cheap or for free because we were being given valuable experience, though I have to say the experience *was* valuable. But it was the money we needed—in my own case, badly. Without it, there was no chance of continuing my education.

Interestingly, both the construction companies and the union with which they bargained seemed to agree that our three-month employment served some higher purpose. Sure, we were kidded mercilessly, but never maliciously or even resentfully. I don't recall anyone ever suggesting that we incompetents, who despite our youth couldn't work as hard as our fathers, should be paid less. Nor did those men seem to resent that, as college graduates, we'd have an easier life and get paid better as well. "Do good," the guys I worked with would tell me each August, and it was clear from their tone that this was instruction, not advice. I'd been granted an unearned opportunity that trailed an obligation. *Do good.* Make the most of the gift. Be thankful. Which I am, truly, and I'd like to think I've done as instructed.

Why, then, do I feel so uneasy to describe myself as a union man? Well, part of it was the union hall. Most summers, my father was able to find me a job wherever he himself was working. It was a done deal by the time I got off the plane. Except, not *quite.* Despite having been hired, I couldn't just report for duty. First, I had to check in at the union hall, let them know that I was there and then wait for the boss's official blessing. Sometimes hours, sometimes days. In my admittedly porous memory the hall was cavernous and murky, weak light streaming in with cathedral effect from high dirty windows, the outer walls ringed with folding chairs occupied by some of the most-dispirited-looking human beings I've ever encountered. In front were offices with fogged-glass windows where the decisions were made and men's lives fucked with. If you were unemployed and looking for work, you went down to the hall early each morning and waited for your name to be called. Maybe there'd be work for you that day, maybe there wouldn't. By midmorning, most days, if you hadn't been sent out on a job, you'd be told to go home and come back the next day. Given how many men were there each morning, the hall was amazingly quiet, but of course that makes sense. Every single one of these guys was waiting for the sound of his name, and if there was noise he might miss it. If you didn't get to your feet right quick, another man's name would be read. Every so often the big guy himself would emerge from behind that fogged glass, and everyone was suddenly alert. Memory is a trickster, but in mine the Albany union chief—fat, jowly and imperious—was straight out of Hogarth, the scowling pawnbroker in *Gin Lane*. Sometimes he'd have a fistful of slips, which he'd hand to another functionary, and then names would be read. Other times he'd just survey the hall and return to his office without a word. If you missed a day, if you stayed home with a sick kid, you could count on being told the next day that your name had been called (whether this was true or not) and asked where the hell you were. Did you want to work or not? To make sure you understood, your name wouldn't be called that day and maybe the next.

When your name *was* finally called, you reported to the jobsite and handed the slip you'd been waiting for to the foreman, who'd likely say, "The fuck do I want with this?" and hand it back. This whole pointless rigmarole always made me absolutely crazy, and every summer I complained bitterly to my father about the breathtaking stupidity of the system, as if it were his fault. What would happen, I'd ask, if I showed up for work without the slip the foreman didn't even want? The look on my father's face then was the same one that guys who did this hard work for a living gave us college boys half-a-dozen times a day: it said, *How could you go to college and be so stupid? What courses are you taking? Next year, try different ones. Learn some fucking thing.* "You had to wait," my father explained, "because you had to wait, *capisce?*" So what if the site foreman didn't give a shit about the slip? That wasn't the point. If you went to work without one, they'd know back at the hall. You can't work on this job unless you're a union guy, and if you're a union guy you go down to the fucking hall and sit there until your fucking name's called, which *is* the fucking point. And if you think there's another fucking point you're sadly fucking mistaken.

Nor was such lunacy confined to the hall. One summer I was hired as an assistant on a carpenters' crew. They were good, hardworking guys who seemed to enjoy having me around and didn't mind showing me what I was supposed to be doing. The problem was that even though there were four of them and only one of me there often wasn't enough work to keep me busy. Construction's like that. Sometimes you go flat-out; other times, until the others finish their task, there isn't a thing in the world for you to do. Part of the job, everyone understands, is looking busy until you actually are. Stand around leaning on your shovel for too long, and somebody's going to come over and tell you to go home.

To me, looking busy was heavier lifting than, well, heavy lifting. *Looking* busy diminishes the soul. Sensing my unhappiness, as well as my curiosity about their craft, my carpenters took me into their fraternity and proceeded to educate me. I learned how to use a level and drive a nail, which done right doesn't go *tap-tap-tap* but rather **bang!** The hammer starts somewhere behind your ear and comes forward with lethal force. If you deliver a glancing blow, the nail flies about thirty feet through the air and hits a real carpenter in the back of the head. And that's fine. Everybody misses the nail now and then, but when you do it's distance you're after. The nail you miss-hit shouldn't land on your own work boot. If the blow is true, the nail is driven all the way in. If not, the second finishes it off. If it takes three strikes, somebody's going to shout, "*Hit* the fucking thing! What're you building over there, a piano?"

"Just watch out for the steward," my carpenters warned, because the kind of education they were offering me was strictly prohibited. If I got caught holding a level or pounding a nail, we'd all be in trouble. The good news was that everybody knew the gray sedan the job steward drove around in, and most of the time we were out of sight behind the massive forms we were building. But of course I did eventually get caught. I heard the wheels of the steward's car skid on dirt and turned to see him coming toward me on the double, his face purple. He hadn't seen me actually doing any carpentry, but I'd stupidly slid a hammer into my belt, and that was all the evidence he needed. He yanked the hammer out and gave it a good, long toss. My carpenters all came out guiltily from behind the form to receive their share of the inevitable ass-reaming. "Don't ever, *ever* let me see another fucking hammer in this kid's belt, you hear me?" he said. Chet, my favorite carpenter, foolishly tried to stand up for me. "All he wanted to do is learn something," he said. "Yeah?" said the steward. "Well, I hope to fuck he just did!" He then turned to me. "So," he said, "you want to be a carpenter? Is that it?" I could see Chet shaking his head no. "Not really," I said, to which the steward replied, "That right there, what you just said, is the correct fucking answer. Say it again, so I know you understand."

I said it again.

"Don't forget it."

By the end of the day, my father, working at the other end of the site, had heard about the incident. Knowing what a hothead he could be, I was afraid he'd go looking for the steward, read him the riot act and get us both shit-canned. "Why would I do that?" he said, when I expressed my concern. "You're the one in the wrong, not him." Since the point seemed worth arguing, I went for it. The essence of my case was both simple and, I thought, unassailable. Since I'd started really working with my carpenters, we'd become a better, more efficient crew. I wasn't shirking my responsibilities as a laborer, just being of use when the guys needed an extra hand. My father was having exactly none of this. "If they need an extra hand," he said, "that means they need another carpenter. Some guy down at their hall's looking for work." I could tell he was reciting the union party line that he only half agreed with, but he was obdurate nonetheless and clearly irritated with me for not being able to wrap my mind around the lesson.

In fact, I was bereft. Lately, instead of dreading work when I woke up each morning, I'd actually kind of begun to look forward to it. The job had become meaningful. I was deeply attracted to any work I could get good at. Most summers I resented being yanked out of the academic life I was trying so hard to belong in. And not just resentful but anxious. Though construction work wasn't complicated—pick up a steel form and toss it on a truck bed—that didn't mean I'd be told how to do it or precisely what was expected of me. What if I failed to catch on? For the first month or so, I'd be an embarrassment to both myself and my father. Yet at some point every summer things pivoted. I'd realize that I *did* understand the job, which alleviated my anxiety if not the crushing boredom. And in my third summer, I began imagining a life. I could see myself wearing a tool belt, having mastered a significant skill, a guy who fit in his work boots, who'd shout good-naturedly at the newbie, "*Hit* the fucking thing! What're you doing over there, building a piano?" Yes, I needed the money. It was absolutely necessary. When it arrived, I was always happy as hell to have it. But it wasn't fulfilling. *Making* something, though, *knowing* it was well made . . . that was a different story.

On the drive home, my father softened. "Whose hammer did you have?" it occurred to him to ask.

"Chet's spare," I said.

"He should know better."

"He did know better. He's a good guy."

"The best," my father agreed, his point being that, at least as far as union road construction was concerned, nothing was more likely to put you in the wrong than doing the right thing.

More than any of this, it was my father who made me an uneasy union man. For most of my young life he'd been a mystery, an aching absence, but now, for the first time, I was beginning to understand him. He'd paid my dues all year so I could work for three months. Though he did twice as much work as

I did, he got the same pay and was treated like a rented mule. What bothered me even more was how he behaved around the bosses. He didn't grovel, exactly, but did act falsely jovial, a hail fellow well met, always wanting to tell a joke to men who clearly didn't want to hear it. A guy who'd fought his way from Utah Beach through France all the way to Berlin still feared the sort of man who could ruin him with the stroke of a pen: lawyers, judges, the strutting ne'er-do-well son of the owner, powerful union officials. The jokes he told these men were intended to place them on an equal footing. What he seemed to want them to understand was that as far as he was concerned there were no hard feelings, though it should've been clear to him, as it was to me, that they didn't give the tiniest little shit whether his feelings were hard or soft. Such mostly unwelcome overtures were clearly a source of confusion even to him. "He's not such a bad Joe when you get to know him," he'd sometimes rationalize, more to himself than to me, even when the guy in question was a total asshole and we both knew it. "Anyway," he'd continue, waving it all aside, "end of August, you'll go back to college." *That* was the fucking point he'd refused to admit the existence of earlier, when I'd been going on about having to wait down at the hall and having to look busy when there was real work to be done, work I knew how to do. You allowed yourself to be treated like shit so you could get the slip of paper that let you work for three months, after which you'd go back to college. And when you were done there, your education complete, you'd never again have to wait for another slip of paper. Or so he believed.

My first academic job was at a Penn State branch campus, where I stayed for three years. The teaching load—eight courses a year, most of them composition—was borderline abusive, especially given that significant scholarship was also expected. Free amphetamines should've been handed out in the dispensary, but they weren't. Worse, the institution was profoundly schizoid. At the local campus level, new hires were given to understand that good teaching was the most important goal. The real power, however, was at the main campus in State College, where department chairs made it clear that *they* were in charge of tenure, promotion and merit raises, and those would be awarded *not* on the basis of glowing student evaluations but on scholarly achievement. What this place needs, I often found myself thinking, is a good union to rattle management's cage.

Be careful what you wish for. My next academic posting was in the Connecticut State University system, which was a union shop. I was skeptical. One of the principal duties of a union is to insist upon a safe workplace, something university professors don't worry about. That not every occupation merits representation is the satirical point of the movie *Grosse Pointe Blank,* in which a hit man played by Dan Aykroyd tries to unionize his fellow assassins. There's a hilarious moment near the end when he and John Cusack (who plays a "right-to-work" contract killer) interrupt a pitched gun battle to join forces against a couple government spooks, Aykroyd gleefully shouting, "Workers of the world unite!" as they blaze away at their common management enemy. The offer I accepted required me to teach seven classes instead of eight, at a significantly higher salary, though some of that would go to union dues, and there was no such animal as merit pay. Still, the reduced teaching load meant more time to write and that was what I was after. With a union at my back, I figured, my professional responsibilities would probably be more reasonable.

Like most new faculty, I had to share an office. My companion—I'll call him Robert—was in his mid-sixties, big and strikingly handsome with a mane of flowing silver hair. He'd grown it long decades earlier when, as a young man, he'd auditioned for the role of Tarzan. One of his colleagues had somehow gotten hold of his screen test, and when department parties grew sufficiently inebriated, this would be trotted out so everyone could do their Tarzan yells as a youthful Robert cavorted through the jungle on a Hollywood soundstage wearing a loincloth.

The other interesting thing about Robert was that he held a split position, half time English, half time physical education, where he coached the hammer throw. He was said to be a good coach, and he might've been, but he was no kind of English teacher, at least not when I showed up. That he still had to share an office, despite being a few short years from retirement, gives you an idea of the regard in which he was held, and he'd earned it. Teaching is difficult, especially if you don't know anything, though perhaps not as difficult as it would be if you gave a shit. Robert didn't. Preferring to sleep rather than actually teach his classes, he would send his students off to the art museum and tell them to describe a painting, then slip the essay under the door when they were finished. Our office had two tall filing cabinets, and he put these end to end, rather than side by side, forming a makeshift wall, so that when students came looking for him during office hours, and peered in through the small rectangular window, they wouldn't be able to see him napping, though of course his snores could be heard down the hall. Since the front of my filing cabinet was blocked by the back of his, I had to move his out of the way in order to file anything, all the more infuriating because his contained nothing but sports equipment. But never mind, it was a better gig—more pay, less work.

Unlike at Penn State, very few faculty here published much or attended conferences, and I could've gotten away with doing that myself. If a man who snoozed through half his classes behind a wall of filing cabinets couldn't be fired, then I certainly could get by doing the bare minimum and use the additional time to work on the novel I'd begun that summer. Unfortunately, I had enough of my grandfather in me to share his dilemma. How do you learn not to care about something that matters? Because good teaching does matter. I intended to quit the classroom as soon as I could afford to, but until then I approached my job as my grandfather did his imperfect skins. Each student, many of them first generation, was a puzzle worth pondering. Speed, carelessness and inattention were the enemy. If some of my colleagues were contemptuous of their students' abilities and doing slipshod work themselves, what did that have to do with me? Not a blessed thing.

There's a difference between democracy and egalitarianism, and no matter how strongly you might feel about the former, nothing's more toxic to the soul than the latter. Too often the promise of a union isn't fair treatment but rather equal treatment. Do you do a good job or a shitty one? Doesn't matter. Your union has fought hard for a living wage, so you'll get it. Everybody gets a lollipop. Occasionally there's an ice-cream sandwich and, boy, does *that* look good after all those lollipops. Who gets the sandwich? The one who does the best job? No, because when "merit" is a dirty word the ice-cream sandwiches are doled out on a rotating basis. After all, who wants to stand up and say, I'm more talented than you are, or I work harder at my teaching than you do, or my scholarship's more important than yours?

Well, anyone who shared an office with the Hammer Thrower would be sorely tempted to make that very case. You'd almost rather there *were* no ice-cream sandwiches than see Robert get one, since when his turn came, you'd have to wake him up and hand him his unearned treat and listen to him slurp it down. *Your* sandwich. Because, yeah, that's how you've come to think of it: as your fucking sandwich.

Am I being unkind? Probably. We all have dreams. We all believe ourselves worthy and deserving, if only the right criteria were applied. Many ungifted people secretly believe they've been cheated out of greatness, and Robert did, I happen to know. The closer he got to retirement, the more determined he was to teach an upper-level class in what he called his "specialty": eighteenth-century literature. Every semester he petitioned whoever was then the department chair, and every semester he was not just turned down but also told why: he was lazy, other people had advanced degrees in the same area, while he'd never finished his MA thesis, his teaching evaluations were abysmal. (That's correct. Even in the most egalitarian of systems, people end up making distinctions. Think of communism.) But Robert continued to plead. If he was allowed to teach just this one course, he'd *become* a good teacher. He'd work hard. His enthusiasm would carry the day.

The year before he was due to retire, he begged yet again. The department chair was a good and kind man. How much harm could Robert do in a single semester? Given the harm he'd already done over a long career, this question wasn't rhetorical. But he'd be doing harm in whatever class he was assigned to, so why not let him retire happy? And so, he offered Robert a compromise. If he really wanted to teach the eighteenth-century course, he'd first have to come up with a syllabus, reading list and detailed lesson plans. They'd go over these materials together, and if everything looked okay he'd get a chance in his final semester.

Poor Robert. It must've been all he could do to suppress his Tarzan yell. He went home that night and wrote the syllabus and decided on the assigned reading. By the end of the week he'd worked up lesson plans. The following Monday he met with the chair, who glanced at the reading list and handed the whole folder back; there wasn't a single story, poem, novel or essay on the syllabus that was written in the eighteenth century. Robert had made the classic high-school blunder, assuming the 1800s made up that century.

Are you ready for the kicker? Robert was our department union rep. Surely you saw that coming?

In "The Getaway Car," Ann Patchett's wonderful essay about becoming a writer, she observes that not many beginning cellists believe they'll be playing Carnegie Hall anytime soon, whereas beginning writers (and I was one of these) *will* often send off early work to *The New Yorker*. It's possible that musicians are just smarter than writers, but a more likely explanation is that playing the cello immediately announces itself as both difficult and foreign, whereas writing feels like an extension of speaking, something we've been doing almost since birth. For whatever the reason, aspiring writers are less gifted than cellists at judging how long it takes to get good. When the relatively short apprenticeship that beginning writers too often anticipate turns out to be a very long one, they become understandably frustrated and resentful. Had they gone to law school, they'd be lawyers by now. Indeed, had they chosen to do almost anything else, they'd be making money instead of hemorrhaging it.

A couple years ago, I asked my pal Jess Walter whether he would've considered self-publishing if it had been an option back when he was learning his craft. He answered without hesitation: absolutely. Jess is a writer of such lush, abundant talent that it's hard to imagine there was ever a time when that wouldn't have been immediately evident to any editor. But of course there *was* such a time, and it's still vivid in his memory. He was married, with a child on the way, and for years had worked as a reporter for a Spokane newspaper and foreseen print journalism's bleak future. If his storytelling was going to bear fruit, he needed that to happen sooner rather than later. In other words, his apprenticeship was not unlike my own or that of any writer for whom marriage, children and substantial debt arrive in advance of the first significant payday as a writer. Like Jess, I'd about had my fill of editors rejecting my stories, often without comment. I didn't just *want* a break, I *needed* one.

The question begged, however, is pretty obvious. How would my career have been different if self-publishing had been an option? How would Jess's? When I asked him, he had another quick answer: he'd probably still be writing knockoffs of his first literary hero, Kurt Vonnegut. Which made me smile because, had I known a single thing about murder or "dames" or urban life, I'd have followed Raymond Chandler down the same mean streets that Philip Marlowe trod in the thirties. There was nothing about Chandler's voice, style or worldview that I wouldn't have happily co-opted as my own, were any such thing possible. But what I found most revealing about Jess's reply was that, without thinking, he'd responded to my question as an artist, not as a businessman. Instead of speculating about whether he would've found success and gotten out of debt a lot sooner, he assumed (correctly) I was asking if he'd have turned out to be a different kind of writer, whether that other writer would have been more skillful or less, whether the voice that emerged with less interference from editors and agents would have been more his own, whether he would have eventually learned to see the world with his *own* eyes—that is, the eyes of the author of *Beautiful Ruins*—instead of through those of a writer he admired but probably could never truly *be*.

The reason we were having this conversation in the first place was that we were both at the Associated Writing Programs conference in Seattle. I was there representing the Authors Guild, and most of the sessions I attended were those that would appeal to young writers. Since the guild's mission is to defend the writing life—or what remains of it—I was curious to learn what the lives of emerging writers were like these days, how their aspirations differed from mine when I was in grad school. Were they hopeful or despairing about writing in the digital age? In one particularly revealing session, four talented young writers, all of whom had recently landed their first book contracts, were discussing how much longer it had taken for them to arrive at this point than they'd imagined it would. Working on their MFA thesis, they'd without exception believed they were closer to living a professional writer's life than they actually were. Nor do I mean to suggest that they were a romantic, unrealistic bunch. They had no illusions about getting rich with their first books. They understood that advances were shrinking, especially for literary fiction. In the last decade or so several large publishers had merged, and others had been purchased by multinational conglomerates, causing a gradual shift toward more commercial titles. The landscape of traditional publishing was contracting right before their eyes. Newspapers were failing, and fewer of those that remained devoted space to book reviews. Fewer young writers were given book tours. So, in the face of all this, why were they still so optimistic?

Well, for one thing they'd been accepted by strong writing programs whose teachers had told them they were gifted. They had also worked hard, and by the time they finished their MFAs, they could see the progress they'd made. If anything, their passion had intensified. If they were still a year away, they could live with that, and they were prepared for that year to be rough. They'd be working on their own now, without institutional support and mostly out of contact with their mentors. The kind of crappy jobs that kept aspiring writers like me solvent back in the day—teaching eight or nine sections of comp at junior colleges or branch campuses—had mostly dried up, so they'd have to settle for even crappier nonacademic ones, but what the hell? You can stand anything for a year, right?

Except it wasn't a year. It was three or four. Nor were the contracts they finally landed with Random House or Viking, but rather a second-tier trade publisher or small press, which meant a tiny advance, no book tour, no advertising budget. To these young talents, this is what triumph looked like in the digital age, and their friends without contracts actually envied them. So, clearly, did most of the recent MFA students in the audience.

In another part of the hotel, during the same time slot, there was another panel, this one made up of indie writers and publishers, and I suspect it was considerably more upbeat. Self-pubbed authors, especially those in the first wave, who were brave and smart enough to see the potential of digital publication and were able to make their names before the inevitable glut that followed, are nothing if not evangelical in their zeal for doing things their way. They see the digital disruption of what they call "legacy publishing" as long overdue and worth applauding. Can you blame them? Before that disruption most of them either had no careers at all or were stuck in contracts with traditional publishers who were unwilling to do for them what they believed they could do for themselves. Now, postdisruption, they finally had a seat at the table, even if it wasn't the grown-ups' table. Why wait three or four years to get a disappointing contract from an old-school publisher when Amazon or another e-book platform could have you up and running by the end of the month? Most of the revenue generated by your self-pubbed e-book would go into your own pocket, not your publisher's, and payment begins almost immediately. Better yet, you get to call all the shots yourself—the cover, the price and where to spend money marketing it. Plus you get to be part of a genuine democratic revolution. And when the day comes that traditional publishing collapses under its own weight, when the snooty gatekeepers and tastemakers are expelled like biblical moneylenders from the temple, you could say you were on the right side of history.

So imagine, you're in that audience listening to these exuberant indie authors. You're married. You've got one kid and another coming soon, mounting debt and a job you hate with every fiber of your being. You believe you have talent but couldn't afford a writing program that would help you find out, or else you just didn't get in. You've tried dozens of agents, none of whom are interested. You know neither the right people nor the secret handshake. You also don't know how much longer you can keep the dream of becoming a professional writer alive. Every passing day erodes what's left of your self-confidence. Self-publish? Make some money? Tell me where to sign.

Yet before you do, a caveat. Because evangelical though they may be, many indie authors also pride themselves on a certain pragmatism. Doing everything yourself, they admit, will not be easy. Yeah, sure, you get to make all the decisions, but a lot of responsibility trails in the wake of that freedom. You have to not only write your book but market it, and the latter (which otherwise is handled by your publisher) takes countless hours and requires skills that not every writer possesses. Which means you'll need to budget enough money to hire the professionals who know how to do what you don't.

If there's a takeaway, it's this. To be successful at self-publication, you have to understand—and most indie writers, like others, as well, are adamant about this—that *writing is a business*. In other words, they have arrived at a very different conclusion from Jess Walter's, when he responded to my question about how his career might have been different if he'd taken this alternate route. For him—and, yes, for me—writing is less a business than a vocation, a calling. Not so much something you choose as something that chooses you, not so unlike a drug, really, in that it's hard to imagine quitting. Whether you'll actually make any money is almost beside the point. Viewing writing as a vocation doesn't make you special, just different. And maybe not in an entirely flattering way. It was Dr. Johnson, after all, who famously remarked that "no man but a blockhead ever wrote except for money."

Most people, an old academic colleague of mine once remarked, are pretty logical. Grant them an initial assumption or two and they'll proceed rationally along a predictable path. If writing *is* a business, like making or selling shoes, then what you're looking for is a workable, efficient business model. If that fails—if the rewards are outweighed by its risks—you'll have to find something else to do, and this, too, will be a business decision. On the other hand, if writing is a *vocation*, like the priesthood, then you'll likely soldier on, economic reality be damned. What you're after is something akin to grace, and where do you go to get that kind of good?

When I got serious about writing fiction, I was finishing up a PhD in English at the University of Arizona, so all I had to do was walk across the hall, knock on the door marked CREATIVE WRITING and sign up for a workshop. Back then the Arizona MFA was a three-year program, though I took only a year and a half to finish it because, as a doctoral student, I'd already fulfilled the program's lit requirements.

I'm frequently asked my opinion of writing programs, often by people who hope I'll trash them and are clearly disappointed when I don't. That said, the landscape has changed since I did my MFA and not for the better. Back in the late seventies, there were only a couple dozen of them, whereas now no university English department is complete without one. In terms of quality they run the gamut from excellent to borderline fraudulent. Nor are they cheap, so if you're thinking about spending that kind of money it's important to consider what you hope to get out of it. I got all anybody could reasonably expect out of mine: competent teachers who could explain what I was doing wrong; role models I could observe as they went about the business of being writers (their habits very different from those of scholars); other apprentices who were as talented (if not more so) and committed as I was, who would give me a push when I needed it and offer the necessary solace of fellow sufferers, which differs from that of your spouse, who suffers because she loves you; and time, which might be the most important. Because a good writing program is a port in a storm, a safe harbor where you are surrounded by people all trying to do the same strange thing, which guarantees that for as long as the program lasts you won't have to explain yourself to anybody—and I can't stress enough how often this happens in the wider world. As helpful as good teachers and rigorous workshops are, the best programs are the ones that provide the most complete refuge. (Apprentices in Renaissance guilds often lived together in space provided by the organization.)

What most programs *don't* offer, though, is precisely what too many apprentice writers are hoping for: connections, introductions, a path to success. When I left with my MFA, I had no agent and only the vaguest notion of how to get one. During my time in the program I was never introduced to an editor. I had little sense of the economics of the writing life. What would be a good advance for a first novel? I couldn't even have guessed. If writing was a business, then my education was sorely lacking. On the other hand, if writing was a vocation, I'd done pretty well. My teachers did me the great favor of taking my work seriously and pointing out my more glaring errors, and on those rare occasions when, mostly by accident, I managed to do something right, they encouraged me. I learned what my tools were for and practiced using them. Maybe I couldn't yet drive that metaphorical nail all the way in with one blow, but I wasn't timidly *tap-tap-tapping* anymore, and since I had a right to my tools (by virtue of having been accredited), I didn't have to look out for the shop steward. My mentors had also given me a sense of the magnitude of the undertaking. The rest was up to me.

Okay, I was lucky and had a good experience, but does it follow that writing programs are necessary? Can't you just rent a cabin in the woods and put in your time? Isn't that what Hemingway advised? In his book *Outliers,* Malcolm Gladwell makes a strong case for what he calls "the ten-thousand-hour rule." Apparently that's about how long it takes for most people to get really good at anything difficult and complicated. One of his examples is the Beatles, who went to Hamburg, Germany, and were contractually obligated to play all night long in strip clubs. Thanks to that incredibly grueling schedule—they played seven nights a week—Gladwell argues that the band that returned to Liverpool at the end of this stint simply wasn't the same as the one that had left. His conclusion: put in the time because genius isn't nearly enough. That wisdom certainly squares with the experience of my own lengthy apprenticeship. I and my fellow aspirants were all reasonably talented, some brilliantly so, but by and large those who logged in the hours were the ones who got good. I was far from brilliant, but I was dogged and came to understand that doggedness will do if it has to. David Foster Wallace, who was in the next generation of writers to go through the same program, was undoubtedly a genius, though it would be a mistake to attribute his success to his brilliance alone because nobody worked harder or with greater discipline than David.

The trouble with Hemingway's cabin in the woods is that it's a cabin and it's in the woods. The Beatles didn't get good by renting a self-storage garage in the boonies and doing their ten thousand hours in solitude. There seems to be an audience component to getting good, even if the audience happens to be in a Hamburg strip club. Yes, young writers need to log long hours with their tools, but once their solitary work's done, they need to talk and compare notes with other apprentices, as well as mentors. With others, they need to test their sense of what's working and what isn't. Hearing even drunken applause is important; it helps you keep going. Even more vital is registering those moments when the audience's attention flickers and the drunks go back to watching the naked girls. It's essential to understand that, unfairly or not, naked girls always have the advantage, and how do you learn that in the woods or sitting alone in front of a computer screen? No, the time to go to that cabin in the woods is *after* you've learned how to use your tools, not before. It's hard enough to imagine characters and a story for them to function in without also having to imagine, with nothing to go on, how an audience is likely to react to them.

My point is that if a writing program won't necessarily make you a writer, you'll still need something like it. Hemingway had Paris and its salons, and he contrived a pretty good workshop there with Gertrude Stein and Sherwood Anderson. The recent debate over whether young writers are better off enrolling in an MFA program or just moving to New York City has been fascinating, but it shouldn't obscure the fact that both address the same need for community during the crucial apprenticeship stage. It's simply not a good time to be alone.

Before I became a full-time writer, I was on the MFA faculty at Warren Wilson College, which, in an earlier incarnation at Goddard College, was the first of the low-residency programs that have since proliferated across the country. The basic idea was simple and brilliant. Many people who want to become writers can't just drop everything and, as the cliché goes, follow their dream. They have spouses and kids and mortgages and forty-hour-a-week jobs. They might be able to steal an hour or two to write most days, but they can't leave home to do it. They need access to professional writers, but not every day. What many of them *can* manage, if they have supportive spouses and understanding bosses, is ten days in the summer and another ten in the winter to attend intense, boot-camp residencies, after which they return home with assigned mentors who will read and respond to their work remotely over the next five months.

This nontraditional arrangement has several advantages. MFA faculty in these programs are culled from other academic institutions that, in July and January, are on hiatus. Often these writers are experienced teachers with the kind of national reputations that would be difficult or impossible to assemble in a single traditional program, and the faculty changes from semester to semester, ensuring variety and freshness of approach. The students are often stronger, too, especially in terms of maturity (skewing older) and hunger. Because time's in short supply, the residencies are crammed with lectures, workshops, panel discussions, readings and individual conferences; the intensity of the experience lingers long after students and faculty return home to their lives and families. I had great students at Warren Wilson, several of whom went on to become professional writers, one or two of them now household names. Yet despite all that, these low-res programs have going for them, they're less than ideal because the refuge offered is brief and the writers, even those who can form fast friendships at the residencies, don't have the extended access to one another that's most helpful. Back home, they can't call somebody from the workshop and suggest getting together for coffee or a beer. All communities, not just writerly ones, thrive on physical proximity. Indie-published writers, sensing this need for community, try to form online relationships and support groups, but these suffer even greater restraints than the low-residency programs. New York City? A standard MFA? The Paris of Hemingway and his pals? They all work on the same principle. You're done for the day? Great. Meet you at Gertrude's. Alice is making brownies.

Writing communities also offer apprentices something they badly need but probably imagine they could do without: myriad opportunities to encounter, decipher, translate and finally comprehend the word "no." When Jess Walter says he wouldn't have been the same writer if he'd been able to self-publish, he means, among other things, that the people who say no to you serve a very useful purpose. The bitter pill they ask you to swallow is medicine. Systematically removing potential naysayers—teachers, agents, other writers, editors—from one's life might feel liberating, but its likely effect is to lengthen, not shorten, your apprenticeship. John Lennon, playing eight-hour shifts in Hamburg strip clubs with his fellow Beatles, must've felt like a slave, and like every slave he must've resented his shackles, but he would've also noticed which songs worked best and which parts of the songs garnered the most applause. Most important, when the drunks' gaze drifted back to the naked girls, he would have heard that silence loud and clear, even over the thunder of his amplified guitar, and understood it as advice: *Stop doing this,* or *Stop doing it this way,* or *Try something else,* because *this isn't working.* The word "no" is the message no artist or craftsman wants to hear: *You're not good enough yet,* which the little voice in your head, the one that lives to fuck with you, immediately explicates as: *You're not good enough and you never will be.*

Writing communities provide the necessary understanding that the word "no" isn't personal; that's important because personal is precisely what rejection (a nine-letter synonym for "no") feels like. When a computer says no—as mine does several times a day—I don't take it personally, unless I'm *really* pissed off. After all, it's just a machine. It's telling me I've done something wrong, which I'd prefer not to be true but invariably is. I've added an extra letter or number or I've forgotten to add *.com* or *.net* at the end of the address, and until I figure that out I'm going exactly nowhere, no matter how many names I call it. I don't take the machine's intransigence to mean that I'll never be any good at operating it or that I'm not good enough in general, either. I just have to find my mistake and fix it, after which, assuming I haven't put my boot through the screen, we can be friends again.

Communities also excel at conveying that there are different kinds of wrong. Most often when you mess something up, the error doesn't go to the core of your being. If you fail a chemistry test, you'll likely locate the problem (as with the computer) in yourself. You should've studied that periodic table harder. Okay, maybe your teacher could've explained things a bit more clearly, or maybe you suspect he doesn't like you, but the answer you gave on the test was wrong, and no amount of arguing is going to make it right. The mere fact that there's another human being involved doesn't make your failure personal. It's your knowledge of the subject matter that's being called into question, not your character, much less your entire essence. Writing a story or poem, though, isn't like taking a chemistry test. Here you *are* offering something of yourself, some part of your inner life, or maybe something you love, and when someone tells you it's not good enough, it feels pretty damn personal. It's a lot like asking a girl out. If she says no and then, in the hopes of not hurting your feelings, adds that it's nothing personal, your first thought is, Hey, it was a person, *me*, who was asking. How can it *not* be personal? Young writers, when rejected, know this feeling well.

One of the beauties of community in general and writing workshops in particular is that the apprentice gets two opportunities to learn: from his or her own mistakes, and from other people's. Back when I taught writing, I always reminded my workshop students that each of them should feel personally invested in every story, not just his or her own. You can't afford to let your mind wander during a discussion of someone else's work, because story problems are pretty common, as are their causes. If you haven't made the same mistake yet, you probably will next week or next month or next year, and probably for the same reasons. Or, put differently, you learn there are a finite number of mistakes and it's best to familiarize yourself with them. The person who wrote the story under discussion today has made you a gift, not just of its strengths but also, especially, of its weaknesses. The cabin-in-the-woods writer derives no such benefit. Granted, in time he may tumble to what he's been doing wrong for so long, and if the cabin's full of books there will be positive examples that can help illuminate him, but seeing how common certain mistakes are and how to go about remedying them makes you feel less alone and less vulnerable. The more mistakes you recognize and correct, the quicker you progress from apprentice to journeyman and, if you're very lucky, to master. And here's the irony: the ultimate purpose of a good workshop is to wean you of its necessity. After a while, like Lennon in Hamburg, you hear the word "no" in your own head every time you play a false note or play the true note at the wrong time or at the wrong volume. You come to understand that rejection, at least for a period of time, is indeed your friend.

"Art," Ann Patchett has written, "stands on the shoulders of craft." You learn first what can be taught. You put in your ten thousand hours. Then you wait patiently for the arrival of what can only come from within: *voice* and its first cousin, *style*. It's worth mentioning that these come last because so many apprentices seem to believe the reverse—that writers are born with a voice they are duty-bound to defend, as if it were an inalienable right. Here, again, the example of the traditional guild is instructive. It's not unusual to find paintings in museums that are attributed to a "school of" rather than a particular artist. The school or guild that produced the painting is recognizable, and perhaps its most famous practitioner worked on the canvas in question, but it's often impossible to say for sure. The clearest sign that a "journeyman" painter—this was a formal guild designation that at the time didn't trail today's negative connotations—was making the transition to "master" was that he began to have a voice, began doing things differently and better than others in the school. That voice hadn't been suppressed by his teachers, but rather coaxed by them into existence. Talent, plus practice (the ten thousand hours), plus time (lots of it) yield voice, attitude, style.

Voice might come well down the line, or even last, but that doesn't stop many critics from inveighing against writing programs, claiming that they stifle, mute, alter or otherwise do violence to the *beginning* writer's most valuable asset. Academic workshops—the argument goes—produce "workshop stories" that are as formulaic as those that appear in genre magazines. Read the blogs of self-published authors and you'll hear this same familiar refrain. Not only do teachers, agents and editors come between writer and reader, their unwarranted intrusions replace the writer's natural voice with something generic and bland and inauthentic. Alas, there *is* some truth to the claim that the sort of fiction encouraged in writing programs is itself a genre—like romance, or sci-fi, or mystery—in the same sense that what we call "standard written English" is a dialect. But that's not really the point. The question is: How does a writer find her voice and arrive at a style that is truly her own and not, as Jess Walter put it, a knockoff? Does a writer find his singular voice by refusing to listen to other voices (so as to avoid being influenced), or does he immerse himself in that Babel of other voices until, counterintuitively, his own somehow emerges? Put another way, does advice from other writers on matters of craft help or hinder the search?

Before addressing that question, though, it's best to pause and reflect on the fact that some excellent craftsmen—painters, poets, writers, photographers, filmmakers—never find a truly singular voice or show much evidence of a distinctive style. Raymond

Chandler had both, and it's not necessary to read more than a paragraph in one of his novels to recognize it. To this day writers try, with varying degrees of success, to imitate his style, but his voice is his alone, as exact and unique as a fingerprint. Nor is voice—at least in the sense I'm using it—necessarily a function of the ear. How much of an Alfred Hitchcock film would you have to watch (even with the sound off) to be confident it's his? Isn't it Caravaggio's "voice," even more than his technique, that makes a canvas of his so recognizable, even at a distance?

Why, then, do some artists find a voice and create a style that is entirely their own, while others, equally talented and hardworking, never do? I suspect it has something to do with what drew them to art in the first place. Jane Smiley has observed that writers fall into two camps: they are motivated either by curiosity or the need for self-expression. She sees herself as belonging in the first group, and her work reveals an intelligence and imagination that is remarkably unfettered. There's very little she isn't curious about, and she loves to try new things. She once said that she hoped to write one of every kind of novel, a goal that would put a premium on flexibility: the artist as shape-shifter. Smiley is one of our finest novelists, and I always pick up a new book of hers with genuine anticipation: What's she up to this time? What I don't immediately feel, or even particularly need, is a familiar, reliable Jane Smiley "world." Her strength is variety, her passion to understand the length and breadth of human experience. She seems content to leave herself largely out of it.

Compare all this with the feeling you get picking up an Elmore Leonard novel, where voice is always front and center. Your immediate thought is, I know this world. I know the man who created it. Unlike Smiley, Leonard isn't interested in everything; rather he's drawn, predictably, unapologetically and obsessively, to certain preoccupations again and again, though the effect isn't so much repetition as familiarity. Since Smiley's books are all experiments, we expect some to be better than others, whereas a Leonard novel promises and delivers something more uniform. You could argue pretty convincingly that, unlike Smiley, Leonard never wrote a truly great novel; either that or they were all great because they were all by Elmore Leonard, his voice ringing perfectly true, time after time, like a church bell.

It's also worth noting that there's a cultural aspect to the great value Americans put on voice. Our deep Emersonian belief in the primacy of the self must be related to our conviction that identity—which reveals itself through voice—is somehow present from the moment of conception, the ultimate trump. This cultural predisposition goes a long way toward explaining why writing is taught so differently in the UK, where, in the destiny sweepstakes, the historical trump has not been individuality but class. Creative writing programs came late to Britain and have never proliferated there as they have here. The British approach to such instruction is both practical and hands-on; they don't seem to worry that strident criticism might do harm to an apprentice writer's voice or self-confidence. For example, a popular teaching tool in England is the "public edit," whereby a story or poem is projected onto a screen and an "editor" (usually another writer) goes through it line by line, cutting out unnecessary words, questioning diction, sequencing, tone and the like. You never choose a deeply flawed story but rather one that feels "close." The story to be edited must evince not only proof of talent but also evidence that the writer is in control of major story elements; character, conflict and point of view are working in concert, scenes and dialogue and narration are used effectively. Despite all this, the story just isn't hitting on all cylinders. It's good, but it could be better, and the public edit is designed to demonstrate how. The process can take anywhere from half an hour to an hour. The author is there in the crowd and is allowed, at the end, to ask follow-up questions, but it's understood that this isn't an opportunity for rebuttal. Little effort is made to psychoanalyze the writer, to discover his or her intent. Rather, the approach is technical. Diction, style choices, flabby prose, transitions, the handling of fictional time—everything goes under the microscope. This is not unlike the piano teacher who places her hands over her student's, or a golf pro who demonstrates the proper grip, stance or rotation of the hips. Nor is it all that different from the technique of a Renaissance guildsman with a promising apprentice. *Here's how you hold the violin; this is how you grip the bow.* The audience for these public edits in England, I'm told, is often in the hundreds, and attendees all seem to understand that the true subject is writing in general, not just the story under discussion. The underlying principle is that every writer faces myriad choices, not only at the macro level of storytelling but also at the micro level of language, choices that over time add up.

It's difficult to imagine such an exercise ever catching on here in the States, where teaching writing is much more hands-off. When I taught at Warren Wilson, for instance, there was a general aversion to "don't do this" proscriptions. The job of the workshop leader was to facilitate discussion of the story or poem, clarify observations, ask leading questions, but otherwise to keep out of the discussion as much as possible until the very end. By unspoken convention the leader sits near the middle of the seminar table, not at its head, because, well, we're Americans, all of us created equal. Though the criticism can be rigorous, the American workshop's emphasis tends to be on constructive suggestions for improving the piece. Moreover, the story or poem is the author's property and is accorded all due respect. The workshop's leader might make recommendations in the margins, or better yet on the flip side of the final page, but you wouldn't cross out whole phrases or replace weak word choices with stronger ones, any more than you'd take a copy of *Frankenstein* out of someone else's book bag and start making notes on the inside cover. Because the Warren Wilson program was so strong and effective, I tried to abide by these rules for my first few residencies, addressing issues of editing in individual conferences, demonstrating how small changes can have a cumulative effect and actually become part of the discovery process of good storytelling. Still, something felt deeply wrong about this concession. I couldn't help feeling the workshop's participants would've profited from a more public exercise, and that the benefits would have far outweighed any discomfort the writer felt for having his sacred prose violated. In subsequent residencies I ignored this injunction completely.

It's an old dispute. Prior to the current debate about whether an apprentice would be better off to enter a writing program or just move to New York City, there was an equally interesting one about cutting one's teeth in journalism (as Jess Walter did). Here, too, the debate had a cultural dimension. A harried, cigarette-stained city editor at a metropolitan newspaper had neither the time nor the inclination to indulge the sensitivities of any budding novelists on his payroll. He'd have no compunction about rewriting your lede, resequencing your sentences, scrawling concrete words above your vague ones or writing *Bullshit!* in the margin of your concluding paragraph, before returning the piece to you with coffee stains on it and telling you to try again. His relationship to you was simple: he'd been doing this for thirty years and knew how; you'd been there for nearly six months and didn't. In this guild hall Carl Hiaasen, Pete Dexter and Joan Didion all found their voices. Hemingway also wrote for newspapers before joining Miss Stein's Paris salon—and before exiling himself to his cabin in the woods, not after.

Which brings me back to rock and roll and hunger. In that now-long-ago junior-high gym, something was revealed that I didn't know existed, something I couldn't live without. At fourteen it doesn't seem possible that you might have more than one such revelation in a lifetime. But what I said earlier is true. I was nearly thirty before my world cracked open again. Nearly finished with my dissertation, I'd taken to writing stories on the side and, before I knew it, was obsessed to the point of addiction. Though an adult by then, I nevertheless recognized that gobsmacked, weak-in-the-knees longing all over again. I felt the same simple imperative: *You* must *do this*. That you have no idea *how* is only one of the many things you will have to deal with. So I walked across the hall and knocked on the door marked CRE-ATIVE WRITING and said out loud that I thought—no, feared—I wanted to be a writer. Need I state that what I'm describing here is not business, not economics?

What either will or won't sustain the apprentice for however long it takes to get good is that visceral hunger. I spent all four years of high school drawing electric guitars I couldn't afford in the margins of my homework and even, sometimes, my exams. Many people my age claim that the sixties were officially over for them when the protests against the Vietnam War turned violent. For me that came when the Who started smashing their guitars at the end of their concerts. To this day I've never forgiven those fuckers for doing that, and I never will. I had several girlfriends in high school and fell deeply, obsessively in love with each one, but it was guitars—sleek and burnished and beautiful—that remained the constant, filling my imaginative margins. I was in college before I could afford a decent guitar, a twelve-string acoustic Gibson with pearl inlay that, when played in front of a good mic, sounded like a goddamn orchestra. Ironically, that was the guitar that taught me what no cheap instrument ever could—that I would never create the music I wanted to. An instrument that's better than the person playing it can have that sobering effect. Almost from the start I'd suspected that equipment wasn't my real problem, and now I knew it for a certainty. I could play and sing okay, and throughout grad school I had a gig, as well as a small following, at the same Tucson restaurant where I gradually, reluctantly and finally acknowledged the gap between my desire and my talent, and that was the end of the affair. Had I stuck with it, redoubled my efforts, been more serious and dedicated, I would've gotten better, just nowhere near good enough. I still remember the fever, though, and even now when Springsteen's guitar thunders and he growls into his mic I glimpse a life other than the one I've got, one where I, too, was born to run. It's a chimera, of course, a distant, ghostly echo of the boy I once was, who had replaced one impossible longing—for an intact family—with another that rendered that family beside the point.

But hunger remembered is not the same as hunger felt. Indeed, for some that's the final cruel joke—that hard-won mastery of craft coincides almost to the minute with passion's ebb. Art, offered shoulders to stand on, often as not demurs.

That art should be so elusive is deeply mysterious. In many respects it seems so straightforward. What art demands of us has remained constant down through the centuries—that we slow down, observe, contemplate, court quiet, practice stillness, live as if we have all the time in the world, knowing full well that we don't. To my glove-cutting grandfather, time was something you spent, not saved. It was a necessary investment, whether you could afford it or not. Yes, joining a guild saved time by allowing him to learn from professionals, but once his apprenticeship was complete, saving additional time meant cutting corners, which no true craftsman can abide. In retrospect, what I find most fascinating is how often his artistic impulses were at odds with his political convictions. He'd fought in two world wars in defense of democracy, something he believed in to the marrow of his bones. He had no great affection for money or power, especially used unwisely or against the defenseless, which was why he spent much of his life opposing the shop owners, who always had things pretty much their own way. In the end, though, they weren't the ones who did him in. Technology did that. Once the clicker-cutting machines came in, there was little need for a man with his skills, his craft. Maybe that's a more significant difference between craft and art. The former is linked to economics more intrinsically than the latter, which makes craft more vulnerable to disruptive technology. Craft isn't necessarily superficial but is often *about* surfaces, the feel and texture of a cowhide, the arrangement of teeth in a human mouth. Art goes deeper and lives deeper, perhaps protected by the surface it lies beneath. Anyway, my grandfather made his choice. He sided with the men who worked those machines by helping them to unionize, and thus became complicit in his own demise.

If art values stillness, quiet and contemplation, commerce has always been about speed (efficiency) and noise (advertising). Commerce, abhorring stillness, demands more or less constant motion. In the glove shops where my grandfather worked, going fast seemed like a good idea because going slower clearly wasn't. Many of today's self-published writers seem to feel this same technology-driven need for speed, which might be why they spend so much online time sharing secrets for greater productivity. One writer of historical thrillers realized that he was wasting valuable time by actually visiting the places where his books were set when most of the information he sought was already waiting there on his computer. "Three books a year is a job," one indie blogger recently sneered, "one every three years is a hobby." By such a metric Donna Tartt—*The Secret History* and *The Goldfinch* each took her *ten years* to write—is the laziest of writers. In that same time frame most indie authors would have written thirty e-books, and readers could have purchased all of them for the price of *The Goldfinch* in hardcover. For many indies, traditional publishing isn't just too exclusive and undemocratic, it's too damn slow. Why, once you finish and deliver your book, should you have to wait nine months or longer for it to come out? Amazon will publish a digital version in a fraction of the time, and they won't make you wait to get paid, either.

The real question for writers emerging in the digital age is how to reconcile what they're doing with how they're doing it. It's a special challenge for those who have aspirations beyond commerce to go slow on platforms designed for speed. I'm not suggesting that art can't be made under these circumstances. Obviously, self-publishing doesn't disqualify a writer from being an artist any more than selling your paintings in Washington Square does. But a writer who doesn't sense the tension between commerce and art is likely to consider any technology that leads to greater productivity an ally. It's also good for the would-be artist to remember that there are worse things than feeling conflicted. If my grandfather were alive today, I have little doubt that he'd see the Internet as a giant clicker-cutting machine whose purpose is to efficiently produce and distribute inferior goods, but he'd also smile at the idea of disrupting the routines of proprietors who've controlled the whole game for so long that they're now feeling cheated out of a future they'd never really earned.

As this essay has no doubt illustrated, I'm every bit as conflicted as my grandfather must've been. Belonging to both the Writers Guild and the Authors Guild, one a union, the other not, I often feel whipsawed between their nonaligned missions. I can write a movie script in six to eight weeks, a TV pilot in four to five, whereas a novel takes me years. Moreover, like my grandfather, my convictions as an artist don't always align perfectly with my politics. I'd prefer every writer who wants a career to have one, even those writers—traditionally or self-published— who don't give a hoot about craft. I might hate egalitarianism, but I'm all for equal opportunity and a level playing field. The secret handshake that many indie writers seem to believe is the key to getting into old-school publishing might not exist (if it did, how would I, of all people, have learned it?), but as Malcolm Gladwell argues in *Outliers*, advantages early on are often magnified over time. For a writer, these include having access to books when you're growing up; or going to the kind of college where you're likely to meet a teacher who inspires a devotion to literature or a classmate who has a parent in, say, publishing; or, later, living somewhere that offers you the chance to join a writers' group; or marrying someone who's able to support you during your apprenticeship.

I also feel—why not admit it?—a proprietary relationship to authorship that's out of sync with both the times and the professional organizations I'm a member of. I'm not convinced, for example, that there's no relationship between my personal health and well-being as an artist and the health of the art I practice. Yes, I'd like for all aspiring writers to be able to achieve a career, but I care more about those who hope to become craftsmen and artists rather than entrepreneurs and businessmen. The whole point of social media, which I assiduously avoid, is to say, *Look at me. Look how many* likes *I have, how many* followers. *I'm important!* The craftsman and artist says the opposite. Don't *look at me.* I'm *not important. Look at my* work. *It's so much better than I am.* But avoiding social media is a luxury I can afford, since my name was established before the Internet itself was invented. Today's emerging writers have little choice but to promote themselves, and many have gotten good at it, not because they want to but because they *have* to. I can't help wondering, though, at what cost?

Of course, the tension between art and commerce is as old as either, but the digital disruption seems to have tilted things, at least temporarily, in the direction of commerce. It's entirely possible that we're now witnessing a gradual evolution away from careful thought, deliberate craft and unhurried delivery. We may have arrived at a consensus wherein the race goes to the swift, the profits to the efficient. If so, it's been coming for quite a while. In 1966, when I was taking the most important academic exams of my life, the tests that would shape my future, all of them were timed. As a slow reader (and, yes, probably a slow thinker as well), I resented that constraint, all the more so because its necessity was never explained to me. Throughout my life I've gravitated to activities where a lack of speed didn't completely disqualify me. A hopeless sprinter, I instead ran cross-country, which requires the runner to keep putting one foot in front of the other, and to keep going after others have stopped. What could be better suited to someone of my aptitudes and liabilities than writing novels, an activity that allows me to feel slow, stupid and even lost for three or four years, provided I somehow figure it all out in the end. It's a profession that allows the slow-footed and dogged to prosper, and you get no additional points for arriving at the destination first.

What we'd all like to know, I suspect, is what happens to arts and crafts when so much else in the culture puts a premium on speed. Do they have to adapt, along with those who practice them? Or does the culture offer an accommodation by recognizing that some things simply cannot be rushed? I remain cautiously optimistic. I see no evidence that people have lost either the ability or the desire to discriminate between what's shoddy and what's well made. If books cease to be what most people my age still think of them as—paper and ink and glue—people will still be hungry for stories. And if e-books were one day to follow print books into extinction, we'd still want narratives. Explaining ourselves *to* ourselves by means of stories is as fundamental as eating and breathing. And despite the noise, we all of us, even those who embrace this digital turmoil, continue to crave the quiet. Last year, curious about the world of indie authors, I entered into an e-mail correspondence with a successful self-published writer. Given the depth and breadth of our very different experiences, this exchange was surprisingly cordial. For him, my absence from Facebook and Twitter and the blogosphere probably reinforced the Luddite stereotype of hidebound writers. For me, his online presence, the sheer number of words he devoted to his regular blog, was every bit as mystifying as my total disinterest in social media must have been to him. When I asked how he managed to keep writing at such a breakneck pace, he told me that the trick was to have an endgame. He'd been at it for too long already but hoped to continue for another year, then come to a full stop. His dream was to sail around the world with his wife. Just the two of them and a bunch of books he'd been meaning to read, and his laptop in case an idea for a story or novel should come to him. No Internet connection, though. Just the quiet. Just the days rolling by to the rhythm of the waves. No hurry.

In other words, to live and work as if you have all the time in the world, knowing full well that you don't.

Address to the Graduates
of Colby College

May 2004

A couple years ago I was talking to a man whose son had graduated the year before from Stanford University. He was proud of the boy, who'd done well there, and also proud that his son had received the kind of education he himself had never dreamed of. But he had misgivings as well. I could tell he had something on his mind that I, as a former college professor, might be able to help him understand. It took him a while before he finally came to the point, which was "Why do you have to mess with them?"

"Mess with them," I repeated.

"Right," he said. "I sent my son off to Stanford a good Republican, and four years later he comes home and tells me he's voting Democratic. You should hear some of the things he says."

"Well, he learned to think," I explained. "If it makes you feel any better, I sent my daughter off to Colby College a good liberal, and by the end of her junior year she was dating the president of the College Republicans."

"Let's swap kids," he suggested. "Yours got smart."

"Not on your life," I told him, though I knew his son well and was fond of him. "What happened," I went on, "was supposed to happen. I mean, think about it. It cost you thirty-five grand a year for four years at Stanford. That's one hundred forty thousand dollars. The kid thought just like you before he left. If he came back thinking like you, you'd have done better to put the money in your pocket and lock him in the house."

But he wasn't convinced. He still wanted to do that swap, I could tell. Weirdly, the whole conversation was vaguely familiar, and after a while I remembered why. In a novel of mine called *Straight Man,* a professor named William Henry Devereaux Jr. remarks that it is the vain hope of middle-class parents that their children will go off to college and later be returned to them economically viable but otherwise unchanged. Hank understands what many parents never quite seem to grasp—that sending kids off to college is a lot like putting them in the witness-protection program. If the person who comes out is easily recognizable as the one who went in, something has gone terribly, dangerously wrong. Indeed, these young men and women we're returning to you today have been so thoroughly messed with—and I don't mean messed up—that you may not recognize them, especially dressed as they are. On behalf of Colby's faculty, I'm pleased to report that it's been fun making their heads spin these last four years. For the most part we're rather pleased with the results, and we hope you will be, too.

But here I am talking to your parents instead of you, the class of 2004. I can tell you can't wait for what I have to say to be over, so I'll try to be brief. In my fifty-four years I've learned very little that I can pass on to you with much confidence, so brevity shouldn't be a problem. Virtually nothing in my life has gone according to plan, and that's the good news, because I'd have settled for far less than I've been blessed with at every turn. With that in mind I have two things to offer today: first, a story, and, second, some advice about the rest of your lives. If you're only able to pay attention to one, listen to the story, because I am by profession a storyteller. I've come to a point in my life where I think almost exclusively in narrative, and as my own fiction-writing students this semester can attest, about the only reliable advice I have to give is on how to make stories more plausible, more moving, more true—in other words, how to lie better. On life, I'm not so reliable.

Anyway, the story. About ten years ago I was teaching at a large midwestern university while awaiting the opportunity to teach at a small eastern liberal arts college, which came in due course. One Friday night my wife and I went to a party given by one of my graduate students in a house that, if it had been a car, would have been a Studebaker up on blocks. The keg had run dry half an hour earlier, a collection had been taken up to buy another, and it had only just dawned on the people at the party that nobody knew the guy who'd volunteered to go get it. In the living room the rickety furniture had been moved out onto the porch to create a dance floor, and Grace Slick was singing "Somebody to Love," a song I've never been able to resist, especially when the volume on the stereo is set on stun, as it happened just then to be. "When the truth is found to be lies," Grace wanted us to understand, "and all the joy within you dies."

Across the room, dancing with free-spirited abandon, was a good-looking young professor of religious studies with whom I'd had a couple of run-ins and never particularly cared for, though she was far too attractive to dislike entirely. She approached life, it seemed to me, with the kind of bitter cynicism that I associate with academics who have come to believe, rightly or wrongly, that they will not be granted tenure. Is it even necessary to add that she lacked a sense of humor? Anyway, at the moment, the young professor's face was lit up from the inside with something I'd never seen there before—joy, unless I was mistaken—and this made me wonder if I'd misjudged her. I hoped this might be true. Did I say she was attractive?

It was maybe an hour later when we professors, perspiring and red-faced from our exertions, and unused to being up after ten o'clock, began to take our leave, so our students could begin the real party. My wife and I left through the kitchen so we could thank our hostess, and there we encountered an intimate and utterly unexpected scene. The professor of religious studies was sitting at the kitchen table, her head in her hands, sobbing pitifully, over and over again, "All I ever wanted was to sing a little rock and roll." Staring at the chipped, beer-soaked Formica tabletop, she'd had a revelation, you could tell. Thanks to Grace Slick she was beginning to see her life in a whole new way. To this point she'd imagined that her problem was that she wasn't going to get tenure, whereas she now saw, to her complete horror, that of course she would. Whatever had lit up her face on the dance floor had been extinguished, and it was hard to believe it would be rekindled anytime soon. In this, her moment of terrible truth, I found myself liking her better than I ever had before, though, with her defenses down, she wasn't nearly so good-looking. Seeing her sitting there, so despondent, you could imagine the effort it took to present herself to the world each morning.

I don't tell you this story today in order to encourage all of you '04 graduates to find careers in the music business, but rather to suggest what the next decade of your lives is likely to be about, and that is trying to ensure that you don't wake up at thirty-two or thirty-five or forty tenured to a life that happened to you when you weren't paying strict attention, either because the money was good or it made your parents proud, or because you were unlucky enough to discover an aptitude for the very thing that bores you to tears, or for any of the other semivalid reasons people marshal to justify allowing the true passion of their lives to leak away. If you're lucky, you may have more than one chance to get things right, but second and third chances, like second and third marriages, can be dicey propositions, and they don't come with any guarantees. This much seems undeniable. When the truth is found to be a lie, you're still screwed, even if you're tenured in religious studies.

The question then is this: How does a person keep from living the wrong life? Well, here are Russo's Rules for a Good Life. Notice that I don't say "for a happy life." One of the reasons the novelist Graham Greene despised Americans was that phrase "the pursuit of happiness," which we hold so dear and ensured, to his way of thinking, that we'd always be an infantile nation. Better to live a good life, he believed, than a happy one. Fortunately, the two might not always be mutually exclusive. Bear in mind that Russo's Rules for a Good Life are specifically designed to be jettisoned without regret when they don't work. They've worked for me. Your mileage may vary.

Rule # 1 Search out the kind of work that you would gladly do for free and then get somebody to pay you for it. Don't expect this to happen overnight. It took me nearly twenty years to get people to pay me a living wage for my writing, which makes me, even at this juncture, one of the fortunate few. Your work should be something that satisfies, excites and rewards you, something that gives your life meaning and direction, that stays fresh and new and challenging, a task you'll never quite master, that will never be completed. It should be the kind of work that constantly humbles you, that never allows you to become smug—in short, work that sustains you instead of just paying your bills. While you search for this work, you'll need a job. For me that job was teaching, and it's a fine thing to be good at your job, as long as you don't confuse it with your work, which is hard not to do.

Rule # 2 Find a loving mate to share what life has in store, because the world can be a lonely place, and people who aren't lonely don't want to hear about it if you are. At some point you're going to tire of yourself, of the sound of your own voice (if you haven't already), and you're going to need someone whose voice you never tire of, someone who'll know you better, in some ways, than you know yourself and who'll remind you who you are when you forget, and also about why things matter. After thirty years, my wife, Barbara, and I continue to delight in each other's company, and that's astonishing given the number of other people we've grown weary of. I have to tell you that the odds of finding the right person to spend an entire life with are not great, and if you get it wrong, badly wrong, your good life will morph into abject misery. In which case, go back to Rule # 1 and concentrate on your work. Maybe she'll go away. Or he.

Rule # 3 Have children. After what you've put your parents through, you deserve children of your own. Next time you're back home, get out the old photo albums and take a good look at some pictures of your parents when they were your age. Talk about the witness-protection program. But don't let these snapshots of your parents when they were happy and carefree dissuade you. Have kids. Don't worry that you can't afford them, though it's true, you can't. Don't worry too much about the world they'll be born into, which will suck, because that's what the world mostly does. You won't be a fully vested citizen until you have someone you love more than life to hand this imperfect world over to. And don't worry that you may have poor parenting skills, which you will. Just remember this: everything you say and do from the time your children are born until the day they move out of the house should be motivated by the terrible possibility that your son or daughter could turn out to be a writer, a writer with only one reliable subject: you. When my father, whom I loved dearly, died over a decade ago, I'm sure he rested easy in the belief that most of the evidence had died with him. There was no chance he could have predicted that one day there would be so many copies of *The Risk Pool* and *Nobody's Fool* floating around, not to mention a major motion picture. Had this possibility occurred to him, I can't help thinking he would've done a few things differently. So, as Carmela Soprano says, "Watch your step." But by all means have children. No one was more aware of the dangers inherent in reproduction than yours truly, and I have two beloved daughters, one of whom graduates here today. They are the pride and joy of my life, and neither of them would ever, ever write about their father, would you, Kate?

Rule # 4 If you have a sense of humor, nurture it. You're going to need it, because, as Bob Dylan has observed, "people are crazy and times are strange." Just as important, remember that in an age as numbingly earnest as this one, where we're more often urged to be sensitive than just, where genuinely independent thought is equally unwelcome to fundamentalists on both the left and right, it's laughter that keeps us sane. Indeed, the inability to laugh, at the world and at ourselves, is a sign, at least to my way of thinking, of mental illness. Mark Twain, overcome by loss and bitterness and despair near the end of his life, did stop laughing, but he never stopped believing in the power of laughter. The angel Satan in *The Mysterious Stranger* fragments, which were among the last things he ever wrote, reminds humans that "against the assault of laughter nothing can stand. You [humans] are always fussing and fighting with your other weapons. Do you ever use that one? No; you leave it lying rusting . . . you lack sense and the courage." Or, as critic Katherine Powers puts it, "We Americans worry about humor, confusing it with a lack of seriousness. [But] look here. Along with art and immorality, it is humor that distinguishes human beings from animals. It is, furthermore, a truly civilizing force, nemesis to the big battalions, and a vexation and puzzlement to the purveyors of mediocrity." And speaking of the big battalions and lethal mediocrity, keep in mind that we are unlikely to vote anyone out of public office who hasn't first been the subject of private hilarity.

Okay, that's pretty much it. This is all I know and then some. Four simple, deeply flawed rules to live by. Go to it. Be bold. Be true. Be kind. Rotate your tires. Don't drink so much. There aren't going to be enough liver transplants to go around.

Good luck.

The Pickwick Papers

Nobody but the author would have blamed Chapman and Hall, Dickens's publishers of the serialized *The Pickwick Papers*, if they'd killed it dead. After all, things were clearly not working out. The first four numbers, despite considerable publicity, had sold on average only four hundred copies. "Pickwick is begun in all his might and glory," Dickens wrote his publishers, before showing them a single word of the first installment, which was later dismissed by critics as a dull, threadbare satire. Worse, the young author was demonstrating that he could be a genuine pain in the ass. The original idea had been that the author of *Sketches by Boz,* which, to be fair to Dickens, *had* caused quite a stir in London, would write another series of sketches to accompany the illustrations of the much more famous Robert Seymour, an artist who specialized in drawing the misadventures of sportsmen. Seymour was to take the lead in the project, providing the story line through a series of humorous drawings. "Boz" would then link these with an accompanying text. But Dickens no sooner agreed to this arrangement (that the artist should lead was by no means unusual) than he thought better of it and proposed, with breathtaking temerity, that things would work better if *he* took the lead and the artist worked to *his* specifications. Also, Dickens felt he needed a much-freer hand with regard to subject matter, arguing that Mr. Pickwick should be allowed to observe whatever he encountered in his travels, which would not be confined to sporting matters. In other words, *Pickwick Papers* would be about what Dickens knew, and not what Seymour knew. Once the project was under way, Dickens further suggested it might be improved if there were fewer illustrations and more text (with a corresponding adjustment in remuneration). Astonishingly, Chapman and Hall sided with Dickens in all of these disputes, and Seymour, understandably stunned and no doubt feeling betrayed, apparently concluded that somebody ought to be shot. Being of a morbid temperament, it was his own brain he put the bullet in midway through the second number of *Pickwick*.

At which point Chapman and Hall must have wondered if their young author was worth the trouble. That's the thing about genius, of course. It *is* worth the trouble. Just about always. But at this point did they know that their brash twenty-four-year-old Mr. Dickens *was* a genius? *Could* they have? Could *anybody* have? After all, the tepid critical response to the first few serial installments of *Pickwick* was richly deserved. The first number, with its tedious send-up of hypocritical parliamentary manners and speech, is the weakest in the entire novel, and given its modest sales by the end of the first four numbers Chapman and Hall must have considered pulling the plug. That they didn't suggests a powerful intuition on their part. They had something in young Mr. Dickens. If they didn't know exactly what, it might prove worthwhile to find out.

They would learn soon enough. With the introduction of Sam Weller in the fourth number of *Pickwick,* the book turned both an artistic and an economic corner. Sales picked up immediately and increased steadily until the original four hundred copies per number had swollen to forty thousand. Even better than the raw numbers was the fact that Dickens was clearly what publishers today would term a "crossover writer"—someone who appealed to both high- and lowbrow, rich and poor, urban and rural readers. Hablot Knight Browne (who replaced Seymour and signed his name "Phiz" to complement "Boz") seemed perfectly in tune with what Dickens was up to. By its last installment *Pickwick* was a full-blown cultural sensation, and London was flooded with "tie-ins": Pickwick hats, Pickwick walking sticks and assorted other paraphernalia. Sadly, neither Dickens nor his publisher had a piece of this ancillary pie, but offers from publishers for other writing projects, big and small, poured in, an astonishing number of which Dickens took on. He had arrived.

Rereading the novel in midlife, I'm amazed at how much of what we associate with the mature Dickens of *David Copperfield, Bleak House* and *Great Expectations* is already present in *Pickwick.* It's truly wonderful to see how sure-handed and confident a writer the young Dickens already was. His subject matter in *Pickwick* is nothing less than England and the English people in a time of radical social transition (just prior to Victoria's reign). Social change is always hard to identify when you're in the middle of it, but Dickens never appears to doubt either his ability to see it truly or to understand the precise significance of whatever he observes. True, as a reporter he'd covered both the courts and the great parliamentary debates, so he had a player's grasp of the issues of the day. And it's true as well that his young life had been rich—more rich than he would have liked—with event. Though he was sheltered and secure in early childhood, his father's spendthrift habits eventually got the family in trouble, landing him (and them) for a time in the Marshalsea debtors' prison. Young Charles, then twelve, fell into dark servitude in a blacking factory, an experience he would never forget and which would haunt his fiction in numerous guises, from *Pickwick* to *Drood*. And later, he had the misfortune to fall in love with the coquettish Maria Beadnell, who apparently toyed with his affections before finally giving him his walking papers and convincing him (like young Jimmy Gatz) that the only way to be worthy of love was to be wealthy and successful. Flannery O'Connor famously remarked that any writer who has survived adolescence possesses enough material to write any number of novels, and this observation seems particularly true of Dickens, upon whom little was lost and less forgotten.

Still, Dickens brought to *Pickwick* a set of remarkably mature convictions, a complex set of values that is—even at age twenty-four—essentially intact. It's one thing to know a lot and to have experienced a lot, but it's quite another to know how you feel about what you've observed and lived. Dickens's "tone"—his attitude toward his material—doesn't develop in *Pickwick* and the early novels; it's already there, rock solid. Witness, for instance, his hatred of social injustice, as evidenced by a judicial system that treated debtors worse than felons. When Mr. Pickwick chooses to enter the Fleet Prison rather than pay an unjust settlement, he encounters there every sort of scoundrel and lazy no-count, but as Edgar Johnson, Dickens's biographer, points out, the writer reserves his most vitriolic contempt for the system itself, which not only allows but actually encourages those with resources to buy their way out of the worst suffering. In *Pickwick,* the law, in Dickens's view, is already "an ass," at least as it's represented by the ignorant Justice Nupkins, the buffoon of a country magistrate, and by Dodson and Fogg, the lawyers who press Mrs. Bardell's meritless case against Mr. Pickwick. Dickens's lifelong conviction that much of what is wrong with British society can be laid at the feet of lawyers would darken and deepen in later novels, where lawyers like Jaggers and Mr. Tulkinghorn hold powerful sway, but it wouldn't change. Present, too, is Dickens's impatience with pretension—intellectual and social. The first makes a mockery of common sense (see the scientific explanation for the "antiquarian" stone bearing the inscription: BILL STUMP, HIS MARK), whereas the second—the sort of social jockeying exemplified by the Misses Nupkins—is not merely foolish but dangerous, since it makes possible the kind of villainy perpetrated by Alfred Jingle, whose understanding that his victims would rather let him get away with his crimes than admit to having been duped, grants him a kind of impunity. And in the person of Mr. Stiggins, who must get drunk in order to ratchet up the eloquence of his temperance lectures, we see Dickens's virulent loathing of religious hypocrisy as well.

Also evident in *Pickwick* are the same positive values that the author would extol throughout his career. Despite his father's spendthrift ways, Dickens would remain a staunch defender of conviviality. That Mr. Stiggins is a drunk troubles him far less than the fact that his inebriated religiosity demands that others withdraw from life's simple pleasures—food and drink—which encourage hale fellowship. The embodiment of such homey virtues, Mr. Wardle, who dispenses so much good cheer at Dingley Dell, prefigures Mr. Fezziwig in *A Christmas Carol,* who each year spends "a few pounds of [his] mortal money" on a Christmas Ball, to lighten the burden of his workers. Nothing is more fundamental to Dickens's secular belief system than the generosity naturally engendered by goodwill, and he insists, here and elsewhere, that lightening the burden of one's fellow humans is not merely the responsibility of governments and institutions ("Are there no workhouses?" Scrooge would later ask) but also of individuals like Mr. Wardle. Sam Weller's introduction in the fourth number of *Pickwick* was important because he not only turned out to be one of Dickens's greatest comic creations but also the embodiment of all that's best, to Dickens's way of thinking, about common English folk. As Peter Ackroyd has pointed out, part of the reason middle-class readers responded so powerfully to the novel was that they saw themselves and their neighbors everywhere reflected. If they were sometimes objects of mirth, never mind: their foibles were human and universal. More important, in Dickens they'd found an author who paid them the ultimate compliment of giving them his attention. He wasn't likely to give anybody a free pass, but they sensed, quite correctly, that Dickens was after bigger game than clerks and coachmen and innkeepers. Oh, he might have some fun with Sam's cockney speech; when he's asked in court how his last name is spelled, he responds that while he's had but one or two occasions to ever spell it one way or the other, he prefers a *v* ("Quite right, too, Samivel, quite right. Put it down a 'we' my Lord," his father calls down from the balcony). And he might also poke gentle fun at the select company of Bath footmen that Sam is invited to join, but in important matters Sam's judgments are sound because he's smart and he understands how the world works. It's not that he can't be fooled. Job Trotter takes him in once. But he can't be fooled twice, at least not by the same person, and that puts him miles ahead of the game in the *Pickwick* universe, which is replete with fools and charlatans. Sam Weller becomes, by the end of the novel, not so much Mr. Pickwick's servant as his caretaker, and, as Ackroyd has tellingly observed, their symbiotic relationship seems to represent a new partnership (of master and servant) for a new England.

And finally Dickens illustrates throughout *Pickwick* his profound belief in the power of laughter. Maybe it can't alter the way the world operates, but the authority of villainy is diminished in the face of ridicule. As G. K. Chesterton, one of Dickens's most perceptive critics, points out, *Pickwick* is the most purely comic of his novels, and the range of the comedy is staggering—from the purely visual delight of seeing Mr. Winkle's horse traveling sideways down the road, encountering the hedge on one side, then the other, to the scathing satire of the riotous, drunken elections at Eatanswill, to the hilarious pomp and pretension of Mrs. Leo Hunter's fancy-dress breakfast—it's all marvelous fun for the simple reason that Dickens himself is always having fun, whether watching people behave or listening to them talk. As good as Dickens is at letting his characters speak directly to us, it's often his indirect discourse that slays me: "As Mrs. Pott grew more hysterical, [she] requested to be informed why she was ever born, and required sundry other pieces of information of a similar description." Often his best laughs, because they're the most disquieting, are edgy and brutal, like Sam's outrageous "Wellerisms": "It's over, and can't be helped, and that's one consolation, as they always say in Turkey, ven they cuts the wrong man's head off" or "now we look compact and comfortable, as the father said ven he cut his little boy's head off, to cure him o' squintin'." Mr. Jingle's disjointed stories display a similar grisly humor ("other day—five children—mother—tall lady, eating sandwiches—forgot the arch—crash—knock—children look round—mother's head off—sandwich in her hand, no mouth to put it in") that we have to assume has its origin in the pure delight of the author more than the character himself.

If the mature Dickens's values are on vivid display in *Pickwick*, so are his particular skills and strengths as an artist. No reader can fail to notice the writer's astonishing energy. He not only creates characters by the dozen but sets them in motion. They ride horses and hang off coaches. They pursue one another in the dead of night. They are discovered where they ought not to be, and they challenge each other to duels. They climb garden walls, get locked out of their rooms, get trapped *in* rooms from which they wish to escape. They eat (we hear about every meal in detail) and drink and blame their hangovers on the salmon, and they seem to rest only in the novel's space breaks. They are thrown out of their lodgings and are forced to find others. Hoping against hope to retain their dignity and avoid humiliation, they are magnetically drawn to the very circumstances guaranteed to provide both. They mishear each other and act confidently (disastrously) on every misperception. Their sheer numbers attest to the fertility of their creator's imagination. Throughout his life Dickens simply could not call characters into being without inviting their families and friends to join the festivities. No sooner do we meet Sam Weller than his father appears on the scene. Another novelist would have been pleased and grateful to have invented Mr. Jingle, but Dickens hasn't time to be either. He's too busy inventing Job Trotter, who completes Mr. Jingle much as Tony Weller completes Sam.

Only when we remember how short Dickens's leash had been, first as a reporter and later as a writer of "sketches," do we fully understand what *Pickwick* represents: it's nothing less than a jailbreak of the writer's imagination. At last he has the scale he needs, and as a result characters and events suggest themselves almost faster than he can accommodate them. He's not writing; he's taking dictation. He's a raging torrent of comic invention. The problem, for the rest of his life, would be control. He would die worn-out, exhausted, ignoring the advice of loved ones to slow down, knowing that he couldn't.

There is also evidence in *Pickwick* of artistic perversity that seems to me somehow central to Dickens's art—a perversity that is, as Poe defined it, "the desire of the soul to vex itself." Novelist David Gates, writing about *David Copperfield,* the most autobiographical of his novels, makes a persuasive case that in Dickens there's often a discrepancy between what he claims to love and admire and what secretly appeals to him. "No matter what he thinks he believes," Gates writes, "Dickens loves Uriah Heep's villainy better than Agnes's virtue." As with other comic writers, it's human frailty and folly that Dickens truly understands and identifies with. But I would also argue that Dickens, perhaps more than any other great writer I know, is genuinely "of two minds." He seems to relish embracing not just the thing itself, but also its opposite, and I've always been fascinated by his ability to slyly undermine whatever position he owns at the moment. To me it's not so much that Dickens doesn't genuinely love, or even truly believe in, the unearthly virtue of an Agnes Wickfield or an Esther Summerson. He just perversely enjoys crafty, fifth-column maneuvers that never allow us to feel entirely comfortable. Two instances in *Pickwick* are particularly worthy of note, I think. The first is the fat boy.

Many critics have pointed out that Dingley Dell represents a kind of Eden: it's lush and beautiful, English country life at its best. Until Alfred Jingle is introduced there, Mr. Wardle's estate is positively prelapsarian, both harmonious and self-contained. But long before Jingle slithers into the garden, insinuating his worldly charms, there's already the fat boy, who in his somnolence, his insatiable appetite and creepy sexuality, is already subtly undermining the very values Dickens appears to extol. The fat boy is, after all, the natural product of an indolent life based on the pleasures Mr. Wardle offers—an abundance of food and drink and hale good fellowship, without work or struggle. "I wants to make your flesh creep," the fat boy confides, and he does. In the background the reader can almost hear Dickens snickering about having so successfully subverted all of Dingley Dell, and we shouldn't be surprised, later, that Mr. Wardle never hears of his friend's incarceration until it's too late to be of assistance. There's a fine interior logic in that, since Dingley Dell exists outside the real world of the Fleet. The Garden, Dickens hints, is not really worth the price, if the price is ignorance.

Nor is this the only place Dickens subverts his own themes. *Pickwick*, readers will note, is a novel of impostors, of people who not only pretend to be what they are not, but also are often, as with Messrs. Winkle, Tupman and Snodgrass, the opposite of what they pretend. Even Mr. Pickwick himself, early in the novel, is feigning to possess an avid intellect, when his behavior suggests he's a dear but gullible old fool. There are so few characters in the novel who are not "false" in some respect that Dickens appears to be placing a premium on both self-knowledge and honest forthrightness. Part of what we like about Sam Weller is that he is what he seems and that he understands himself too well to make false claims. The problem is that this is also true of Dodson and Fogg, who never pretend to be anything other than the sharp swindlers they are. Thus honesty and self-knowledge would appear, in this broader context, to be neutral qualities at best. Conversely, Jingle, the most "false" of all the major players in the novel, who wears identities like changes of (other people's) clothes, possesses a great many traits that Dickens clearly admires—wit, imagination, energy. His smirking disdain for conventional virtue is not just convincing, it's fun. He does everything but moon Pickwick and Wardle when, full of righteous indignation, they pursue him by coach over the English countryside, all the way to London. The only unconvincing (and disappointing) thing Jingle ever does in the novel is to reform, as a result of Mr. Pickwick's kindness. His conversion may seem forced, but here as elsewhere Dickens seems to require opposing gestures. He is himself both a man of genuine faith and the sly, insinuating fellow who cannot resist a natural sympathy for the devil. He proclaims, his voice clear as a bell, his belief in us, in our best selves, then whispers: "Pleased to meet you. Hope you guess my name."

Yet if Dickens brought all this knowledge, experience, wisdom and craft to the *Pickwick* party, there was also much he couldn't bring. He didn't know, for instance, how to write a novel. Oh, he knew what a novel was. Described by biographers as a boy who read while other boys played, he'd always been a voracious reader—of Fielding, Smollett, Defoe, Cervantes and others. But as any writer can testify, reading a thousand novels is very different from writing one. More to the point, when he began *Pick-wick*, Dickens had no reason to believe he'd *need* to know how to write a novel, since that was not what he'd contracted with Chapman and Hall to produce. What he'd agreed to write was a loose, rambling grab bag of sketches. The interpolated gothic tales wedged into *Pickwick* hint at just how loosely the narrative reins were being held. Their relative frequency in the first third of the book further suggests that Dickens may have believed he'd have urgent need of them in order to meet his ambitious word requirements of each installment. That they appear less and less frequently as the novel progresses reveals Dickens's gradual realization that he wouldn't need that particular safety net after all, but even more significant, as the novel moves inexorably from the peace and security of Dingley Dell to the Fleet Prison, Dickens discovered a new strategy. In the early going the darkness of the interpolated tales had balanced the prevailing light of the main narrative, but as *Pickwick* evolved and the primary narrative itself darkened more organically, no such artificial balancing act was necessary. The author learned to integrate, as he would in all of his later novels, its light and dark elements. Having committed to the device of the interpolated tales, he couldn't dispense with them entirely, but he reduces their frequency as the need for them diminishes. By the time we're not quite halfway through the book, both we and Dickens are suddenly aware that he's writing a novel; he's begun to plant narrative seeds that will bear fruit in later chapters, to defer dramatic payoffs and in so doing increase their power.

All of which is evident in the plotting of the *Bardell v. Pick-wick* lawsuit and trial, the continuing story of Mr. Stiggins and Tony Weller and the various romances of Sam, Mr. Winkle and

Mr. Snodgrass. But the best evidence of Dickens's understanding what this novel must deliver is seen in the character development of Mr. Pickwick himself, who begins as a simple figure of fun but then, like Don Quixote, seems to have surprised his creator by evolving into something more. Early in the novel Mr. Pickwick is often referred to as "the great man" in circumstances that make clear the intended irony of this appellation. Such phrases are gradually dropped, and they disappear entirely by the end, because by then Mr. Pickwick has actually become a great man. Unlike Jingle's unsatisfying transformation, which happens too efficiently (and largely offstage), Mr. Pickwick's is more gradual, more earned: he learns from his travels, from the Bardell/Pickwick lawsuit, from his acquaintance with Sam Weller, whose worldly wisdom opens his master's eyes, even as his devotion strengthens Mr. Pickwick's faith. But it's the Fleet itself—everything that Mr. Pickwick experiences there—that completes his moral education, that causes him to withdraw from further "adventures," to finally act his age. His reluctant admission to Sam—"I've seen enough"—is the novel's moral center, much as Huck's famous declaration "All right, then, I'll go to hell" is the fulcrum upon which *Huckleberry Finn* turns. It's the moment when *The Pickwick Papers* achieves its status as a novel, as well as when Dickens becomes, clearly and undeniably, a novelist. There would never be any doubt from this moment on. He would continue to learn—all artists do, throughout their lifetimes—but he would never again learn at this breathtaking pace. *Pickwick* might not be Dickens's greatest novel, as Chesterton believed, but its pleasures and delights are myriad, and none more thrilling, I think, than the spectacle of genius recognizing itself.

Imagining Jenny

I

Jenny had been given to understand she'd have a private hospital room in which to convalesce. The next day she'd be operated on by Dr. Eugene Schrang, who'd pioneered "gender reassignment surgery," a term that still cracked me up (if it didn't work out, you'd be reassigned again, this time to the motor pool). I don't know if Schrang was the one who actually came up with the idea of using a penis to create a vagina, of turning one highly sensate organ in upon itself to produce another, but if so, he gets points for imagination in my book. Either that or he just lived through the Depression and, like my maternal grandmother, hated to waste anything. He was also very expensive, though, as Jenny herself pointed out to me, if you're in the market for new genitalia, you really don't want to shop in the bargain basement. Still, I had some doubts about the good doctor. His website featured a giant vagina on its home page, and I'd begun to think of him as "Big Pussy," like the character on *The Sopranos*. One thing was for sure. He had a thriving practice. Dr. Schrang did some eighty male-to-female gender reassignment surgeries a year, and June had apparently been a particularly busy month. When we arrived in Egypt, Wisconsin, he had a wardful of post-op transsexuals, which meant that Jenny would have a roommate.

Her name was Melanie, and she couldn't have been more encouraging to Jenny. "Don't be scared, hon, you're doing the right thing," she counseled in a southern drawl from behind the drawn curtain that divided the room. Pay no attention to that man behind the curtain, I thought, wishing I could whisper this advice to Jenny, who shared my devotion to *The Wizard of Oz*. Over the last two years there'd been plenty of tense, strained moments in our friendship, and lately we clung to laughter like drowning men [*sic*] to an inner tube. It usually wasn't long after an argument that I'd get an e-mail from Jenny that would restore our equilibrium. One such said, "Russo. I've come up with a title for Larry Fine's autobiography. It's *Moe, You Bastard, You Bastard, Moe, You Bastard*." Reading it, I found myself grinning ear to ear, and not just because at age fifty-three I still took pleasure in the Three Stooges. It was, of course, how Jim and I had communicated right from the start—that is, elliptically. To be Larry Fine was to be poked in the eye, cuffed in the head, knocked down, ridiculed and buffeted by a malicious force of nature over the course of a lifetime, and never to know why. By the time you came to writing your autobiography, all you'd know is that you'd had enough. Moe, you bastard.

Melanie's operation had gone well enough, but her recovery had been dicey. Since her catheter had been removed, she explained to us, disappearing into the small bathroom located on Jenny's side of the curtain, she actually had to stand on the commode to pee. When the door closed behind her, we could hear the seat drop and Melanie climb aboard. "It's worth it, though," she assured Jenny ten minutes later as she limped back to her own bed, bathed in sweat from the fruitless exertion. "It's *so* worth it."

In what sense? is what I wanted to ask, but instead bit my tongue. Jenny, herself in a hospital gown now, was beginning to look panicked, all too ready for the sedative she'd been promised. Grace, Jenny's wife, sat down on the edge of the bed and took her hand. "How do you feel?"

"Terrified," Jenny admitted, her voice all but inaudible. "Brave. I couldn't do this without you." Her eyes shifted, kindly, to include me. I searched for something to say, failing utterly, and not for the last time in Egypt. It was language—easy, thoughtless words between friends—that I'd most felt the loss of over the long months. We value our friendships in part, I suspect, according to their ease, and Boylan and I had hit it off from the start. Ten years earlier he had been the very first visitor to our rented camp on Great Pond, where we were staying until we could find a house in Waterville. He'd arrived, bearded then, with a six-pack of beer by way of a calling card, to welcome me to Colby College after I'd been given a job he himself had applied for. He might have been coming to check me out, much as you'd look over the guy your wife left you for, but by the time we shook hands I knew this wasn't the case. By the time we drank half of that first beer, our feet up on the railing of the deck, before I read his two sad, hilarious companion novels—*The Planets* and *The Constellations*—about souls adrift in the wide universe, I knew I'd made a friend. Here was a man (I thought) who spoke my language, to whom I would seldom have to explain myself, who was

predisposed to give me the benefit of every doubt. By the time
we finished that beer, we'd formed, it seemed to me, an unspoken pact, the exact nature of which we'd figure out later, the
details being unimportant. It'd be easy. And until recently it had
been. Now, though, I had to watch every word I said, especially
the pronouns, not because Jenny got upset when I messed up
(she never did) but because my mistakes, especially public, social
ones, caused her both pain and embarrassment. Worse, such
blunders were evidence that I missed my old pal Jim and wanted
him—and our old, thoughtless ease—back again. Which I did.

"You know what?" Grace said later, when we left the hospital
in search of whatever the town might have to offer for dinner.
"She's going to get *all* the good drugs. We're not going to get
any."

Barbara, my wife, happened to be away visiting family when
Jim told me. She returned a couple days later, and I drove down
to Portland to meet her evening flight. We'd spoken a couple
of times, but I'd said nothing about Boylan because it wasn't
the sort of news you impart over the phone and also because I
myself had only begun to process what I'd been told. The first
person I always want to tell important news to is Barbara, partly
because I can trust her reactions, which are often more generous
than my own, and partly because I often don't know what I truly
think about things until I *do* tell her. Which was why it now felt
so strange to possess knowledge that I badly wanted to conceal
from her. I waited until we'd loaded her luggage into the trunk
of the car, gotten through the worst of the Portland traffic and
safely onto I-95 pointed north, and only then, when the other

cars fell away and the tall, dark pines began to enclose us, did I lean forward, turn off the radio and tell my wife to prepare herself for a shock. ("This is not about us," I hastened to assure her, fearing she might leap to some terrible conclusion.) As I told her that our friend Jim Boylan believed himself to be a woman; that he'd understood this to be the case all his life and was only now discovering the courage to admit it; that Grace knew and was, of course, devastated; that he'd consulted doctors who had diagnosed his condition; that he intended to enter into a "transition" from male to female—from Jim to Jenny—that would involve hormone therapy and, quite possibly, gender surgery, Barbara said nothing until my voice finally fell. Then she said, "Oh, this is just insane. There *has* to be something else going on. We *know* this man." She was looking over at me now, though it was very dark in the car, as if I, too, at any moment, might be revealed to her as a stranger. I understood all too well what the news was doing to her. What she knew—what she *knew* she knew—was being challenged. The ground beneath her feet had shifted, was no longer stable. Of all the couples we knew, the Boylans had the marriage most like our own, and if Grace had not known the truth, never even suspected it, then what in the whole wide world was truly knowable? If you can be so wrong about something so fundamental, what could you trust? Or, more to the point, who?

We drove on for many minutes, adrift in time and space. I speak here not in metaphor. We were supposed to have gotten off the interstate at Brunswick and taken Route 1 up the coast to Camden, but I'd missed our exit. I know now that this is what must have happened. At the time, though, we were simply flying down the pitch-black interstate, peering out the windshield at a newly unfamiliar world. It occurred to me that what I'd told my wife—that none of this was about us—wasn't true. It *was* about us.

II

Over the long months that followed, as Jim confided in more and more people, it became clear that, as one friend remarked, he'd become a walking Rorschach test. As he revealed who he was, we revealed who we were as well, and in doing so, I suspect, surprised ourselves almost as much as Jim had. When Barbara and I talked about it—and it was impossible not to—we often ended up clinging to each other, reassuring each other that everything was okay with *us*, that we *did* know each other, that we weren't harboring some terrible secret capable of atomizing our marriage should it ever come to light. But every now and then I'd catch Barbara regarding me strangely (or, more likely, I'd imagine her doing so) and immediately conclude that she'd been thinking about Jim and Grace and the fact that nothing in the world was quite so certain as she'd once imagined.

When things spin out of control, when the familiar becomes suddenly chimerical, our instinct is to restore order. Jim's sister, conservative by nature and efficient by habit, immediately set her own world aright by telling her brother she wanted nothing further to do with him. Problem solved, order restored. For the rest of us, encumbered by decency and affection, it wasn't so simple, though I suspect most of us, in our own ways, also would have preferred "the problem" to go away. Looking into our crystal balls, we concluded there was no hope that Grace and Jim's marriage could weather a storm of this magnitude. Sure, they loved each other, were devoted to each other, but they would end up divorced. Thinking of Grace, we decided that sooner would probably be better than later. She was going to have to invent a new life, a new happiness, and the sooner she got started on this necessary task, the better. It was Jim we always imagined moving away, to New York or Washington, some big city where he would find "a support group" of people who had themselves survived their own transsexuality or were in the process of doing so. Interestingly, we didn't immediately see ourselves as Jim's natural support group, nor did we imagine that Grace would be the one to move to New York or Washington, because that scenario did nothing to restore order to *our* world.

My own Rorschach reaction to Jim's revelation was both surprising and disturbing because it revealed an emotional conservatism in my character I'd have surely denied had anyone accused me of it. After the day when Jim first trusted me with the truth and I'd promised always to be his friend, I started wondering if I'd made a promise I wouldn't be able to keep. Almost immediately, I began to feel like Nick Carraway after Gatsby's murder; I wanted the world to be "in uniform and at a sort of moral attention." Jim had explained, and at some level I even believed, that his was a medical condition, not a moral one, but I discovered I was unable to sever that medical condition from its moral consequences. When I asked myself if he (I had not yet even begun to think of my friend as "she") didn't have the same right to the pursuit of happiness as anyone else, my response was no, not if it meant Grace's *un*happiness, not if it put their children at risk. He'd *made* his choice when he took Grace, to have and to hold, until death. "Conduct," Nick Carraway says, "may be founded on the hard rock or the wet marshes but after a certain point I don't care what it's founded on," and I agreed, almost proud that my tolerance, like Nick's, had found a limit. My friend's moral duty was to be a man, in every sense of that term. I tried to imagine myself telling him this. Saying the words: *Be a man.*

Of course my emotional conservatism, if that's what it was, had more than one source. I was not just a recovering Catholic and, as such, prone to see the world in moral terms, but also a fiction writer, and no matter how liberal a writer's politics may be, the act of storytelling is not an inherently liberal enterprise for the simple reason that storytellers believe in free will. A plot, I used to remind my students, is not merely a sequence of events: *A* followed by *B* followed by *C* followed by *D*. Rather, it's a series of events linked by cause and effect: *A causes B,* which *causes C,* and so on. True, a person's (or a fictional character's) destiny might well be more than the sum of his choices—fate and luck play a role as well—but only scientists (and not all of them) believe that free will is a sham. People in life—and therefore in fiction—must choose, and their choices must have meaningful consequences. Otherwise, there's no story. Jim's medical condition—his insistence that it was a medical condition and nothing more—was pure fate; if what he claimed was true, then his circumstance was preordained, which removed the whole thing from the realm of narrative, and doing so ran contrary not just to my residual Catholicism but also to my novelist's sensibility.

Jim himself was a novelist, a fine one. As Professor Boylan of Colby College he, too, had sought solace and understanding in narrative. Not surprisingly, he'd been attracted to imaginative literature, the heroic quest, which so often involves a revelation of the hero's true identity. Only when the hero thoroughly understands who he is can his final dragons be slain. Such stories, of course, are not the only ones in Western literature that deal with transformation, and just as Jim had been drawn by his circumstances to a certain type of story, I found myself compelled by my own toward another. Probably no people embrace change more enthusiastically, at least in theory, than Americans. Who we are at birth is less important to us than who we will become. We are expected, indeed obligated, not just to be but to become. This, in a nutshell, is the American Dream. But we are also by nature a cautious, pragmatic people. After all, Gatsby's need to transform and reinvent himself is his downfall. We are, Fitzgerald suggests, what we are, regardless of our need to be otherwise. Ironically, this was what Jenny herself kept reminding us of, though she was applying the wisdom differently.

I wish I could honestly say it was exclusively great literature I turned to for understanding, but the truth is that I was equally attracted to more lurid, archetypal fictions, especially in the language of film, which has for decades provided numerous cautionary parables of transformation, of men who turn into wolves, into vampires, even into insects. Often these stories are about not only the man who is being transformed but also the faithful, loving woman whom his transformation will inevitably endanger. At the climax of these stories the "creature" must choose between what he's become (a monster) and what he was (a man, someone's lover). His beloved might ask him to deny his new nature, to remember who and what he used to be and to be a man again. In these stories it's always clear that the creature is not to blame for his cruel fate. He didn't ask to be bitten by the wolf, the vampire, the spider. He cannot make himself human again. Rather, the man he was is still "in there," and it is to this former self that the heroine appeals. *Remember,* she begs him.

Remember me. Remember love. Do not harm me. Even now, changed though you may be, you have a choice.

Such is our credo. As social and natural scientists continue to erode our *belief* in free will by revealing the extent of our genetic and cultural programming, novelists continue to hold people accountable for their actions and the consequences of those actions. This is the fiction writer's manifesto, because without it there's no story.

III

Jenny's operation seemed almost an anticlimax. For her it was a natural conclusion—a resolution, really. She wasn't "changing genders" or "becoming a woman." She's always been a woman. A skilled surgeon was simply going to help her move about in the world. If the surgery was scary, well, all surgery is scary. Even for Grace, Egypt wasn't as dramatic as I'd imagined it would be. For her, the point of no return had come and gone incrementally, undramatically, over the long months during which she'd come to understand that this operation was going to happen because it had to. Also, as if to suggest that nothing all that momentous was occurring, the operation itself went without a hitch. Jenny'd been wheeled into the operating room singing "I'm Gonna Wash That Man Right Outa My Hair" and come out clutching a button that controlled her intravenous pain medication. (Grace had been right: Jenny did get all the good drugs.) Within two hours of being wheeled back into her room, she'd talked to her mother and several friends who'd called to find out how the operation had gone. Her voice didn't have much strength—over it we could hear Melanie moaning quite clearly as she stood atop the commode on the other side of the bathroom door, but she laughed and joked on the phone and clicked her button, and by the next morning had no memory of any of it. She seemed, more than anything, very, very happy. "Jim was always the golden boy," Grace remarked wistfully when Jenny nodded off into another morphine dream. "And Jenny's going to be the golden girl." From inside the bathroom came the sound of Melanie climbing down off the commode, then she herself emerged without a flush, suggesting that again no business had been conducted.

You had only to look at Melanie, now haggard and frightened and dispirited, to know that she'd never been a golden boy and wouldn't be a golden girl either. She'd not had a boob job to go along with her GRS, as many transsexuals did when hormones left them flat chested, and as a result did not look, post-op, much different than she had a year before when some guys on the basketball court offered to kick the shit out of her because she looked like a girl. She claimed to be content with an androgynous look, but I had my doubts, since she also admitted to having spent very nearly her last dime on her surgery. She'd come to Egypt alone, as indeed she'd managed her entire transition. Her family and friends, after organizing an intervention in the hopes of preventing her from going through with the operation, kept belittling her right up to the moment she boarded the plane and continued, incredibly, even now, to call her at the hospital to belittle her further.

As a result, she was starved for human kindness and attached herself not just to Jenny, a natural ally, but more surprisingly to Grace and me. The sliding curtain that divided the room and stayed closed when we first arrived was now thrown open so, when we visited, Melanie could be part of the conversation, which among other things helped take her mind off the fact that she couldn't pee. "They're not going to let me out of here until I can," she confided sadly, as if she'd spent her entire life disappointing people as a man and was now doing the same thing as a woman. She'd been scheduled to be released from the hospital the day before and had no idea how she'd be able to pay for the additional stay, not to mention the several outpatient days she'd be required to spend at a nearby hotel, the same one where Grace and I were staying.

For me, Melanie, like the other transsexuals on the ward, posed a paradox. They might not look much like women, but I had little trouble thinking of them as female, whereas Jenny, who could (and did) pass for a woman anywhere, even before her surgery, still seemed like my old pal Jim in drag. As I regarded the two of them in their adjacent beds, I began to suspect that I might be lacking in imagination, the quality that, as a novelist, I was proudest of. No doubt one of the reasons I was among the first people Jim confided in was that if anyone was equipped, by both training and inclination, to understand his plight, it was a friend who also happened to be a novelist, whose stock-in-trade was moral imagination. The problem is that the transgendered person's experience is not really "like" anything, and Jim was to discover, alas, that no one would have more trouble imagining what he was asking us to do than his closest friends, and that my being a novelist counted for less, at least in the beginning, than either of us could have guessed. It wasn't that I wasn't able to imagine anything, or that my imagination had taken a holiday when confronted with intractable reality. Quite the opposite. From the start I discovered myself to be in imaginative overdrive. During the first week, my new imaginings were so powerful and relentless that I had trouble sleeping. Though I knew Grace was a strong woman, I imagined her shattered as she watched her husband disappear, like an old photographic image, into terrible blank whiteness. I imagined their children ridiculed in the school yard, told by adults that they were no longer suitable friends for their own children. During this period, I was working on *Empire Falls,* a novel about the awful weight that kids today have to bear, and it wasn't difficult to imagine Luke and Patrick, thus tormented, driven darkly inward, like my fictional victims, by things they could not explain, even to themselves. And far worse scenarios, too. The Boylans lived out in the country, and it was easy to imagine them awakened in the night as rednecks in pickup trucks with the windows rolled down, full of last-call courage, bellowed their unsolicited opinions into the still night. As well as three-in-the-morning night terrors that were only slightly less lurid than werewolf tales, crammed full of "respectable," real-world violence. Gradually, all these went away.

But as I regarded Jenny and Melanie in their adjacent beds, I realized that banishing phantasms isn't the same as imagining a happy ending, something I'd somehow written off as impossible from the start. I'm not talking here about the sort of happy ending that makes everything all right, that negates loss, that squints at reality in order to substitute a fantasy. Rather, the *qualified* happy endings that my friend and I had always managed to eke out in our own novels, akin to what allows Huck Finn, after witnessing just about the worst that human nature has to offer, to "light out for the territories" armed with little but his own hard-won decency for a moral compass, as fine and true an ending to a comic novel as we're ever likely to see. That's what Boylan and I were, after all—comic novelists—and comic novelists traffic in hope. More important, this was the kind of imagination that Jim had asked of me from the start, and what Jenny required of me now. She needed those who loved her to share her ridiculous, buoyant hope for her future, for the future of her family. The problem was, I not only hadn't imagined a hopeful future for my friend, I hadn't really begun to imagine Jenny herself.

IV

A couple days after the surgery, Grace and I began taking turns at Jenny's bedside. The tiny hospital room accommodated two visitors only if one of them stood, and having two at the same time was also more tiring for Jenny, who, whacked-out on painkillers, felt the need to entertain us. So Grace and I would both drop by in the morning, then I'd leave the two of them alone, returning an hour or two later to take a shift while Grace grabbed something to eat or returned phone calls.

When I returned to the hotel from lunch one afternoon, there was a voice-mail message. "Don't forget to check on Melanie," Grace reminded me. The day before, Melanie had finally peed and was rewarded by getting discharged from the hospital. I hadn't forgotten. Actually, after lunch I'd taken a stroll through town and picked up a couple of things for her at the drugstore. When Grace had spoken to her earlier that morning, Melanie had complained of a headache and a terribly parched throat. Could we stop by later with some lemon candies? Well, of course we could. "We" was, to my way of thinking, the operative word, and since Grace was just then at the hospital, there was no "we" available, just "me." I was already late for my afternoon shift at Jenny's bedside, having dallied over lunch and spent too long talking to my wife and daughters on the phone. If I went directly to the hospital, I could spend a couple hours with Jenny, give Grace her break and then "we" could drop by Melanie's room before having dinner that evening. *That* had been my plan.

Melanie's room was right across from the elevator. I pressed DOWN, and then, while awaiting the elevator's arrival, went over to her door to listen for sounds. Music, the television, anything. If she was sleeping, I told myself, Melanie needed the rest more than the bag of hard candy I held in my hand. I paused, considered, then finally knocked. Behind me the elevator dinged, and when the doors opened a middle-aged couple got off and smiled at me—rather quizzically, I thought, as if trying to connect someone like me with the sick transsexual they'd seen wheeled into 302 yesterday. *Just dropping off this bag of candies,* I wanted to explain as they slipped their key card into the door to 304. Inside 302, still not a sound. I'd done my duty, had I not? I could tell Grace I'd stopped by the room, knocked and gotten no reply. Melanie was either resting or she'd gone out for a walk. Except she hadn't gone out for a walk. She was still far too weak for that, and I'd knocked loud enough to wake her unless she'd been sleeping very soundly. I knocked again.

Unless *she'd* been sleeping very soundly. Odd, but I hadn't slipped with Melanie, never once referring to her as "he." I'd goofed twice with Jenny just that morning. My only consolation was that Grace still messed up occasionally herself. Even so, was this stubbornness on my part? A refusal to let go, even now, of Jim? To all appearances, Jenny had been, these many months, a woman. People who didn't know she'd been a man were slack-jawed with amazement to hear about it. Now, postsurgery, she was anatomically female as well. Between me and full acceptance stood only geneticists and fundamentalist Christians, two groups whose wisdom I'd never before paused in rejecting. It was clearly past time for me to jettison what was holding me back, the midwestern, Nick Carraway–style desire to see the world stand at moral attention that, when allowed to thrive unchecked, turned otherwise decent people into someone like John Ashcroft, the attorney general, who couldn't bear to be in a room with a statue of naked Justice, who had to cloak her lest she corrupt him, poor, pathetic boob that he was.

These were my thoughts when I heard, finally, a stumbling movement behind the door to 302. When it opened, I took a quick, involuntary step backward. The woman who stood framed in the doorway was Rochester's mad wife, down from the attic, barefoot, her hair wild, her eyes frantic and unfocused, clad in a thin nightshirt.

"Melanie?" I croaked, but her eyes had rolled back in her head, and she slumped, first sideways against the frame, then forward into my arms.

V

Story endings, I used to tell my students, are often inherent in their beginnings. In the year that preceded our journey to Egypt, I'd found I was able to imagine the past—that is, to imagine the young Jim Boylan before he and I had met. True, my initial reaction to my friend's news might have been, as I said, conservative, but I soon discovered I had little patience with people who were more sternly moralistic than I was when they learned of Jim's situation. When someone asked how he could have kept such a secret from Grace all those years ago, I realized I knew the answer. As I said, to the novelist, life—whether fictional or real—is a series of dramatic moments, and this was one I had little trouble imagining. Jim, tormented since childhood, and diagnosed with a condition he flatly refused to accept, one day meets the very woman he's been dreaming of and praying for, the woman who frees him from himself. For the first time in his life, he himself simply doesn't matter anymore. *She* matters. She isn't merely Grace, she is *his* grace—a gift from God that can never be earned, only freely and gratefully accepted. Perfectly radiant, she is not just the love of his life, she is his cure. When she smiles, he can feel what he's always regarded as his illness melting away. It's not just women's clothes he gathers together from his closet for disposal before he proposes marriage, it's a shameful self that can now be shed *like a suit of clothes.* Not just hidden out of sight, but swept clean away.

Who *cannot* imagine such a moment? The weight of the self vanishing completely, *banished* by the power of longed-for love, the promise of family, of normality. Does he tell her about the clothes—or the self—in the dumpster? To do so would be to suggest that maybe those clothes aren't really gone, that the discarded self might one day reemerge, and is to doubt the power of the love he can feel coursing through his veins, routing the virus, making him well. What patient doesn't want to believe the treatment has worked, that he's clean, that he can now live a normal life? But to tell his beloved that he's been ill for a very long time, that the illness might return, even though he's convinced it never will? And to tell her now, when his faith, which has never flagged since he was a child, has finally been rewarded? No and no again, and it's in his *not* telling, surely, that we recognize our shared humanity. This is what I attempted to explain to people, barely containing my annoyance that any such explanation should be necessary.

But of course it begged a question. If I could imagine the past with compassion, why couldn't I breathe hope into an imagined future?

It was Saturday, but Dr. Schrang was in his office, and he answered his own phone. "Rick," he said, sounding pleased. "Of course I remember you."

"Melanie's in bad shape," I told him. "She's burning up."

"Put her on. Let me talk to her."

"Well, that's the thing. She keeps passing out. Also, she's sort of hallucinating."

"That doesn't sound good."

Well, do you think it could have something to do with the fact that you cut her dick off last week? I didn't actually say this, just thought it.

"Bring her over," Schrang suggested. "Let me have a look at her."

"I don't have a car, Doctor," I reminded him. *Also,* I wanted to add, *this is not my transsexual. This is a whole other transsexual than the one I came here with. Jenny Boylan is mine. This one's yours.*

"Use the hotel van," he advised, perhaps as an alternative to slinging Melanie over my shoulder and walking the half-dozen blocks through traffic. I hung up and told Melanie, who was now stretched out across the bed, her eyes twitching, I'd be right back. She groaned.

There was a young man behind the desk in the lobby. "I'm going to need your help," I told him, and my expression must have revealed that I was dead serious, that I wasn't giving him an option, that he wasn't going to enjoy the task I had in mind for him, that I knew it didn't belong on his job description any more than it did on mine. "We're going to need a wheelchair, and you're going to want to pull the van right up outside the front door. Room 302," I added.

He seemed to know what that meant.

To my surprise, Grace was in the waiting room half an hour later when I came out of Schrang's office. "I realized after I left the voice mail that it wasn't fair to ask you to do it alone," she said. She'd been to the hotel and heard what had transpired there.

"I almost didn't," I confessed, feeling the chill of that truth.

Later in the afternoon we abandoned Jenny altogether in order to visit Melanie in the emergency room. A massive infection was the diagnosis. But Grace suspected there was more, and she was right. That morning Melanie had gotten yet another phone call from home, from a loved one who wanted her to understand that she was now a freak. Already feverish and shivering and light-headed, she'd been about to call the hospital. Instead she drew the curtains against the harsh sunlight, crawled under the covers and went to sleep. In another couple of hours, her kidneys might have failed. "I could've died," she told us. "If it hadn't been for the two of you . . ."

When Grace went over and took her hand, she broke down. "My partner," she sobbed, "she's not a bad woman. This is just so hard for her." Incredibly, she seemed not to comprehend that the woman she was confiding in knew precisely how hard it was. "But my friends," Melanie went on, looking more like a frightened little girl than a woman, "I don't understand why they have to say such terrible things. Why do they have to make me feel like this, over and over?" She was regarding me now, as if I might know the answer to that one. I thought about the advice I'd nearly given my friend. *Be a man.*

And suddenly I was as angry as I could remember being in years. Angry at those friends of Melanie's who'd allowed her to come here alone, because of course it was easy to be angry at them, having never met them. And angry at Jenny's sister, also for not being here where she belonged, and also because I'd never met her either. Even angry at Melanie herself for being so oblivious, for thinking she needed to explain to Grace how hard it was for the wife of a transgendered person to accept her loss. And, I had to admit, angry at myself for not once having fully imagined how afraid and lonely Jenny had been throughout much of her life. I'd grasped it intellectually, but somehow I hadn't *felt* it until I saw that fear and loneliness reflected in the eyes of a stranger. And finally angry at the whole brutally unfair world, which distributes its blessings and burdens so unequally. Moe, you bastard.

Back in Jenny's room, we gave her the good news (that Melanie was going to be okay) and the bad (that after one blissful day in a hotel room, Melanie had requested to move back into her old room with her old roomie). "If that's okay with you," the nurse added.

"Of course it is," Jenny said, as if the question were absurd, as if people were never unkind, or intolerant, or selfish, or ignorant, as if she'd heard as a child that people could act like that but had never witnessed such behavior personally. It was, of course, the same generosity of spirit, neither masculine nor feminine, that Jim had shown in welcoming me to Colby College, to a job that should have been his, the same generosity that for too long had made him suffer alone rather than share his burden, that allowed him to forgive, again and again, those who trespassed against him. Against *her*.

And so, an hour later, Melanie, looking sheepish, was wheeled in, and we again pulled back the sliding curtain so we could all be one big happy family.

VI

According to Flannery O'Connor, the fiction writer's material falls into two categories: mystery and manners. The latter are, for the most part, comprised of observable human behavior, and often socially constructed (like gender, some would argue), while the former constitutes the deeper truths of our being. These we often keep secret, because to reveal them makes us vulnerable. To my mind, an even-deeper mystery than the secrets we keep is how our hearts incline toward this person and not that one, how one soul selects another for its company, how we recognize companion souls as we make our way through the world in awkward bodies that betray us at every turn. This is not the special dilemma of the transgendered person; it's all of us.

Two days after Melanie returned to Jenny's room, Grace and I boarded the plane that would take us home. I had less than twenty-four hours before I was to embark on a long, grueling book tour. Grace was returning to work and the children and a life she was reinventing, a life she'd *been* reinventing now for nearly two years. As she stared out the window at the flat midwestern landscape below, I regarded her with wonder. Years earlier, her heart had inclined in the direction of another soul, and now, against the advice of many friends and well-wishers, she'd had the wisdom to understand that when our hearts incline—often in defiance of duty, blood, rationality, justice, indeed every value we hold dear—it's pointless to object. We love who we love. In the past two years, for Grace, everything had changed and nothing had changed. Her heart was still so inclined, as was its habit.

The same was true for Jenny. I'd witnessed this earlier in the week, the night of her surgery, at the end of the very long day she'd been envisioning, in one way or another, for forty years. She'd been slipping in and out of drugged sleep all afternoon and evening, awakening with a joke to tell and then falling asleep again in the middle of its punch line. Finally, as it got later, she grew serious. Time, she knew, for Grace and me to return to the hotel. When her eyes filled with tears, Grace went around the side of the bed and took her hand, leaned down and kissed her on the cheek. "Grace," Jenny whispered, "sing me a song." As she began to sing "Two Little Boys," a lullaby she often sang to Luke and Patrick at bedtime, her voice sweet and low, the words themselves inaudible to me, I'd found myself backing toward the open door. Jenny was gazing directly into Grace's eyes, Grace into Jenny's, and their intimacy in that moment was so wholly unguarded that I felt myself to be an intruder. At the doorway I stopped, though, unwilling, and perhaps unable, to leave.

What I was witnessing, I realized, was a great love story. Jenny had told me, many times, about how he—the boy Jim—had walked beneath the Surf City pier when a storm approached and there prayed for love to save him. Gazing at the tableau before me, it was hard to ignore the possibility that this prayer *had* been answered—ironically, of course, as our prayers are answered all too often, the result perhaps of our not understanding what to ask for, or how to ask for it. And it occurred to me too, that if this *was* a great love story, I had no idea where we were on its time line. For all I knew we might be nearer its beginning than its end. How was it that I'd failed to imagine a scene like the one I was witnessing? Was it so implausible? Hadn't I seen this same love and tenderness throughout all the years I'd known these lovers, for that's clearly what they still were, in the sense that mattered most. Is it the fact that the world so often disappoints us that makes hope seem so far-fetched? What makes imagining the worst so easy? Is it really so much more plausible? Or, frightened children that we are, do we imagine the worst as a kind of totemic magic, in the hopes of fending it off in reality?

When the lullaby was finished, Jenny, still holding Grace's hand, looked over at me. She was visibly exhausted, no more than a second or two from deep sleep, though a small impish smile creased her lips. "Russo," she said. "Sing me a song?"

It was a joke, of course, which was just as well. Sing? I could barely speak.

What Frogs Think:
A Defense of Omniscience

Part of the difficulty of teaching anybody anything is that mastery, once achieved, often induces amnesia and impatience in equal measure. Having arrived at understanding ourselves, we no longer recollect what we were confused by or what was causing that confusion. Driving a stick shift, for example, feels intuitive after you've got the hang of it. Your left foot knows where to find the clutch, when to depress it, when to let up and how fast, when to slip the stick out of one gear and into the next, where the various gears are located, where you should be looking when all this happens (at the road, *not* the diagram helpfully provided on the ball of the stick, *not* on the floor beneath the dash where the clutch was the last time you looked, before it moved so that you can no longer locate it).

My father taught me how to drive a stick one summer afternoon when I was home from college. He was not a gifted teacher. After missing the length and breadth of my childhood, he was coming to parental tutoring (and to me) pretty late in the game and clearly wasn't cut out for it. Part of it was that once *he'd* mastered anything, he no longer considered it to *be* difficult. That was how he characterized anything he *hadn't* mastered. Driving a stick, he told me that afternoon, was something any goddamn idiot could do. Half an hour later he had to pick up this gauntlet so carelessly thrown down and admit he was wrong. There was one goddamn idiot who couldn't manage to learn, no matter how loudly the instructions were bellowed at him. I seemed to be wired in parallel. When my left foot came off the clutch, my right instinctively left the gas, stalling the car; conversely, when my left foot depressed the clutch, my right depressed the gas, causing the engine to shriek. To make matters worse, he'd started me off at the base of a steep hill, his rationale being that I would encounter hills eventually and he didn't want my instruction to be deficient in this regard. Worse yet, the vehicle I was learning on was one of his customary beaters, its muffler attached by a wire hanger, with seat springs punching up through ripped vinyl and no power steering. Naturally, its gearbox was slippery, and I kept locating reverse by accident, grinding the transmission frightfully. I can still remember my father's frustration at this most unnatural of mistakes. "Jesus Christ," he complained. "Can't you *feel* it?"

And there's the problem in a nutshell. We do things, especially complicated things, by feel. In familiar situations the wrong thing feels unnatural. Right feels right; wrong feels wrong. To be a novice, we forget, isn't to be ungifted, just unfamiliar, and usually not with one thing but rather a cluster of them.

The omniscient point of view is like that. I haven't made a scientific study, but my sense is that professional writers opt for omniscience far more often than novices, this despite the fact that, once mastered, it's probably the most natural way to tell a story, the virtual default mode of both the eighteenth- and nineteenth-century novel. Years ago, back when I was teaching creative writing, I used to give my beginners some exercises in point of view, just as I did with the other fundamentals of storytelling: character development, conflict, dialogue and tone. My students were required to write the first page of the same story from several different points of view. I'm not talking about changing the point-of-view character from Janice to Bob, but rather altering how the story is told, from, say, first person (*Call me Ishmael*) to third (*He told people his name was Ishmael*). Before making the assignment I explained the core options: first person literary (the narrator seems to be writing, not speaking), dramatic monologue (speaking to an implied listener), close third person, effaced, omniscient and (grudgingly) stream of consciousness/ interior monologue, as well as the seldom-used second person. After explaining how these worked in theory, I asked students to give three or four a test drive. Same story, same characters, begun in the same place. The difference is not *what* we see, but *how*. (Though they quickly learned that *how* often influences and alters *what*.)

Because beginners, like magpies, are drawn to anything flashy, my students were anxious to try the relatively rare dramatic monologue; they'd all read *The Catcher in the Rye* and remembered the effect of Holden Caulfield's idiosyncratic spoken voice. And despite my warnings, they were also attracted to stream of consciousness, which appeals to their inner pretentions even as it appears to offer license for incoherence. They like the effaced point of view because they don't have to enter their characters' thoughts and close third person because it seems to be a hedge against the dreaded workshop question, *"Whose story is this?"* And they enjoy first person literary because they like the sound of their own voices. But omniscience? No takers.

Okay, fine, they're beginners. What about more seasoned apprentices? One winter when teaching in the Warren Wilson MFA Program for Writers, I canvassed the efforts of thirty-five talented graduate-level fiction writers. How many, I wondered, would select the point of view favored by Fielding, Dickens, James, Trollope, Hardy, Chekhov and Tolstoy? By my reckoning, just four. I didn't count stories that began with an omniscient paragraph, then zoomed in, camera fashion, to close third person and never zoomed back out again; I did count those that were clearly *attempting* omniscience, even though it leaked away at times, only to return later, unexpectedly, according to authorial whim. Only four out of thirty-five. That statistic alone might have been meaningless except that several of these stories seemed to be crying out for omniscience. One featured three brothers taking turns attending to their dying, comatose father in the hospital. The author had decided to tell the story in the form of notebook entries, each brother recording his thoughts about their father at the end of his shift. The story built nicely to a satisfying emotional conclusion, and the workshop consensus seemed to be that it was reasonably successful. More than one reader, however, remarked that the notebook entries often felt cumbersome and that the author seemed to be struggling with the problem of how to release pertinent information. How old were the brothers? What did each do for a living? Where were they living now? Were they married? Did they have children? And there were "housekeeping" issues. Whose job was it to describe the hospital room where all this was taking place? The brothers have no reason to describe it for one another, any more than they have any reason to mention their age or birth order. It's the *reader* who needs to know these things, and there didn't seem to be any obvious means of revealing them.

Since we'd identified these problems but offered no remedy, I asked how the writer might have told the story differently, allowing for easier, more natural access to the necessary information. One person suggested appointing one of the brothers the czar of such matters, but this idea was quickly rejected because it skewed the story's symmetry. Whereas before, the three brothers were given more or less equal time, implying they were equally important, you'd now have one who was clearly ascendant. Somebody else suggested letting the dying father provide the necessary personal information about the siblings and let the notebook entries be secondary, thus maintaining the story's balance. Yeah, okay, but wouldn't that solution diminish the brothers collectively? Also, comatose people perhaps aren't best suited to dispensing relevant facts. Well, how about one of the nurses, someone threw out in desperation, causing several others to groan. Nurses have even less reason than patients and visitors to describe hospital rooms, and how would a nurse be privy to information about the brothers? Another dead end, and impatience cloaked the room. (Had my father been there and known the answer, he'd have said, "Jesus Christ, can't you *feel* it?") Could anyone, I repeated, think of a natural way to tell the story that would surrender necessary details about the brothers and the setting and the situation, without upsetting its equilibrium. "Well," someone said, "I *liked* the notebook entries." Translation: *Can we move on, please?*

Obviously, what I'd been hoping for was that someone would

see an omniscient narrator as a possible solution. To be clear, I wasn't advocating omniscience, which might have trailed its own set of problems. And while the notebook entries wouldn't have been my choice for how to tell this particular story, they might still be the author's best option. Maybe it wasn't quite working, but I could see how, with some tinkering, it might. The workshop's purpose is not so much to fix problems as to identify them. Fixes are the author's business. No, what troubled me was that omniscience, for many talented apprentice writers, doesn't even show up on their radar. So you wonder why.

Before I speculate about that, let's define terms. Here are stripped-down examples of the three major third-person points of view that every beginning fiction writer learns. *Bob kissed Ellen.* (Effaced. We don't know what either character is thinking or feeling.) *Bob kissed Ellen, but he was thinking of Sue.* (Close third person. We go into the thoughts of one of the characters.) *Bob kissed Ellen, but he was thinking of Sue, and Ellen was thinking of Tom.* (Omniscient. We access the thoughts of more than one character.) As even this vastly oversimplified summary makes clear, omniscience allows the writer to know more and therefore to reveal more. But no one wants to write a sentence that feels at once clunky and bare. It must be more than freedom we're after. To find out what, let's have a look at a passage from the late Jon Hassler's novel *Grand Opening:*

The moment he set foot in homeroom, Brendan was offered a stick of gum by a shifty-eyed boy named Dodger Hicks, who had been lying in wait for a friend. Among the twenty-four boys and girls of the seventh grade, Dodger had not even one friend, the parents of Plum having warned their children away from him because his father was a convict, his mother drank, and Dodger himself stole things from stores—crayons, comic books, candy.

Dodger was older and taller than the rest of the seventh grade, having taken nine years of school to get there. A poor reader, he was taunted for what his classmates assumed was stupidity and had spent every recess and noon hour of his life lingering at the edge of a game. His face was dark, his cheekbones prominent. He had a habit of nodding his head when he spoke, and of squinting and showing his long teeth when he listened. His dark hair, which hung unevenly about his ears, he trimmed himself, using a pair of small shears pilfered from art class. As he gave Brendan a stick of gum . . . he said he had stolen it that morning from Kermit's grocery, the door being unlocked and no one inside.

"That's our store," said Brendan. "My mother and dad bought it."

"No kidding?" asked Dodger. He gave Brendan the rest of the pack.

The first thing to note about Hassler's omniscience is its immediate, effortless access to the story's information, as a result of which Dodger Hicks leaps to life. We not only see him standing there, "a shifty-eyed boy," in time present but are also privy to his past, to the very events in his young life that have made him shifty—and to the fact that he has no friends and the other children have been prejudiced against him by their parents. We know that Dodger steals things, and what and why. He's swiped a pair of scissors to cut his own hair, an intimate detail that powerfully suggests other sad realities: that in his family there's no money for haircuts and nobody cares enough about him to cut his hair. Thanks to the omniscient narrator's ability to transcend time, to examine both Dodger's present and his past in the same short paragraph, we learn an amazing amount about the boy very quickly. No other point of view provides such efficient access to things the reader wants to know. For contrast, have a look at the opening of *The Great Gatsby*.

In my younger and more vulnerable years my father gave me some advice that I've been turning over in my mind ever since.

"Whenever you feel like criticizing any one," he told me, "just remember that all the people in this world haven't had the advantages that you've had."

He didn't say any more, but we've always been unusually communicative in a reserved way, and I understood that he meant a great deal more than that.

Having described his characteristic tolerance, this first-person narrator, Nick Carraway, admits that it has its limits:

Conduct may be founded on the hard rock or the wet marshes, but after a certain point I don't care what it's founded on. When I came back from the East last autumn I felt that I wanted the world to be in uniform and at a sort of moral attention forever; I wanted no more riotous excursions with privileged glimpses into the human heart. Only Gatsby, the man who gives his name to this book, was exempt from my reaction—Gatsby, who represented everything for which I have an unaffected scorn.

The purpose here isn't so much to begin the narrative as to establish its reliability. This is done primarily through Nick's voice, which comes across as honest, introspective, mature. He lets us know that the story he means to tell didn't happen yesterday. He's had years to reflect on what happened when he was back east. And he's left us something to chew on as events start to unfold: How can someone who represents everything for which the narrator has "unaffected scorn" nevertheless escape his—and presumably our—moral judgment? The first two pages of *Gatsby* (along with the concluding paragraph) have become so iconic that it's hard to imagine anyone reading them and wishing Fitzgerald had opted for a different point of view, including omniscience. We trust Nick Carraway implicitly not just to report events truthfully but to help us understand their meaning. Indeed, we believe him so completely that we probably don't register until later that his perspective is far from ideal. Though he'll be telling Gatsby's story, they aren't old friends. In fact, Nick will be acquainted with Gatsby for only a period of months, and his knowledge of the other man's past is mostly based on hearsay. As the novel progresses we can feel its author chafing against his narrator's inability to convey necessary information. Explanations for how Nick came to learn things after Gatsby's death are sometimes strained, occasionally tortured and, at other times, absent entirely. I don't mean to suggest that Fitzgerald came to regret inventing Nick Carraway to tell Gatsby's story, only that the reader can see how in certain respects he was hamstrung as a result.

Nor am I suggesting that *Grand Opening* is a better novel than *The Great Gatsby,* just that Hassler's omniscience is truly a thing of beauty. After school, Brendan lets Dodger tag along home with him. There he examines all of Brendan's toys, including a boomerang that the younger boy has been unable to make return. Dodger has better luck.

The boomerang sailed up and away, spinning as it climbed, and at its apogee—incredibly high and small—it tilted almost vertical as it wheeled around and began its return flight, picking up speed and spinning faster and faster and heading straight for their heads and passing over them as they threw themselves flat and crashing through the kitchen window. At the sound of breaking glass, Dodger was up and running. He never glanced back or said goodbye.

The noise woke Grandfather, who called from his window upstairs, "Where are we, lad, and what was that noise like a china closet tipping over on its face?" This being Grandfather's second awakening in this unfamiliar house, he was of the opinion—as he had been for a while this morning—that he and his wife and two daughters were lodging in a tourist home en route West, retracing a trip he had made in 1921 to visit relatives. At breakfast it had taken three cups of coffee and a stern word from Catherine to convince him this wasn't a stopover in Billings.

"We live here," Brendan shouted up at him. Then softer: "And my friend broke a window."

"We live here?"

"Plum! Remember?"

Grandfather backed away from the window, smartly rapping his skull with a knuckle—usually a sign that a surge of fresh blood was making a swing through his brain and carrying off his delusions.

His brain function restored, Grandfather recalls his long life as a railroad brakeman:

Treacherous work. He had seen a brakeman killed one icy afternoon in the St. Paul yards. His own freight was pulling out, heading west; he was standing on the rear platform of the caboose and looking off to his left at another freight pulling in. He saw a brakeman standing on a cattle car of the inbound freight. The man wore a long black coat and black mittens. He noticed Grandfather and waved, and then as he turned and was about to leap the gap between the cars he slipped. Down he went, striking his head on the coupling and then dropping to the track, and the wheels of the cattle car passed over his legs, or rather passed through them, for they were cut clean off just below the hip. Grandfather, riding away, signaled his engineer to stop and he jumped from his caboose and ran through the sleet to the other train, which continued to move, wheel after steel wheel rolling over the bloodsoaked pants and coattails. Grandfather pulled the man away. He was out cold, had been knocked out before he hit the ground, thank God. Grandfather waved and shouted but the train continued to crawl through the yard, and when the caboose finally rumbled by, there on the back platform stood the second brakeman looking down in disbelief at his dying partner, whose loss of blood was so lavish it spouted like a fountain from his stumps and he lost his life before he came to.

Ah, the damn trains. The wonderful damn trains.

How effortlessly the narrative baton is passed from one character to the next here. The action moves gracefully from Dodger to Brendan to Grandfather without any of the devices required by more limited and limiting points of view. No new chapter or even a space break is required. Nor is any explanation for the shift needed. One moment we're told what Brendan is seeing and thinking as the boomerang returns, and the next paragraph relocates us to Grandfather, a whole new character and consciousness. Again, the outside view enables us not only to know his thoughts but also to evaluate them (as delusions).

Notice, too, that being unrestricted by time and space has the effect of encouraging digression. Yes, the story of the man dismembered by the train can be viewed as part of Grandfather's personal history, but the ease with which that lengthy incident is worked into the larger narrative is worth pausing to admire. In the novel itself it's followed by two other, equally vivid train stories, and while you could think of them as illustrating *Grandfather's* passion for trains and a lost way of life, the original source of that passion is clearly the author's. Hassler knows a lot about trains and train lore, and he's chosen a point of view that allows him to indulge an enthusiasm that predates his invention of Grandfather. After all, "omniscience" means "all knowing," and it favors writers who know things, who are confident of their knowledge and generous enough to want to share it.

Where does such confidence and generosity come from? Some writers, like Dickens, appear to be born with it. To others it comes over time, a side benefit of experience. One thing I'm pretty sure of is that the more confident and generous a writer becomes, the more he will be drawn to omniscience, often out of frustration with more limiting points of view. My own second novel, *The Risk Pool*, is a father-son story told from the son's first-person perspective, its first two words "My father." I don't remember giving the matter much thought. I just began the story in a manner that felt natural. I was probably a little more than halfway through the first draft when I really became aware (like Fitzgerald, I suspect) of the limitations of first person. Because I was writing from the son's point of view, I had no direct access to the father. As the writing progressed, I grew more and more haunted by how different the story would have been if I'd allowed the father to speak in his own defense. I wanted to *know* about him, not guess. Hadn't I spent most of my own young life speculating about my father's motives based on woefully incomplete information? No doubt I wanted greater access to the father in my story because I'd craved that very thing with my own. I didn't feel like I'd chosen my point of view unwisely, just that those first two words trailed serious unintended consequences.

By the time I finished the first draft, I'd pretty much decided that my next book would also be a father-son story, this time told from the former's point of view. Indeed, I started *Nobody's Fool* the day after I finished *The Risk Pool*, determined to explore everything I couldn't get at in the earlier book. Understand that I wasn't opting for omniscience, just a different first-person narration. But immediately there was a problem. No way this novel was going to begin with "My son," or for that matter "my" *anything*. Sully, my new main character, wasn't an introspective guy, and it would never occur to him to tell his own story. He was too busy living his life, which was hard physical labor and a series of barstools. So, close third person, then. The book would be *about* Sully. We'd have access to his thoughts and feelings, to what's going on in his present life but also to his past. For a while this worked better. The deeper I got into the story, though, the more I sensed that something wasn't right. Like my own father, Sully was all kinds of fun to hang out with, but he didn't understand himself very well, nor was he terribly interested in learning how to. The few conclusions he'd come to about his life were very different from the ones I was discovering. He seemed to believe his destiny was ruled by luck, and I simply couldn't agree. In close third person, though, it wasn't possible to register my dissent. I'd located myself inside Sully so I could see the world as *he* saw it. My logic had been that I would have access to all his experiences, thoughts and memories. That was all well and good, but it also meant that anything else would be off-limits. Realizing this, I immediately wanted *out*.

I still remember that feeling of panic. I wanted out? What did that even mean? That Sully wasn't interesting enough as a character to support a whole novel? Or that I'd somehow failed to adequately understand him, to get at his core? These are very dispiriting misgivings to harbor in the middle of a first draft. To me they suggested, in the famous words of that NASA official when the *Challenger* blew up, "a major malfunction." Just as troubling as my doubts about Sully was the fact that one of the book's minor characters, Miss Beryl, his landlady, was commanding more of my attention than I'd anticipated. The old woman, who was not modeled on anyone in real life, revealed herself to me with greater ease than Sully, who was based on my own father. Should I give her freer rein and see where she led me? What if I began the book with her?

Worth a try, so I began the book yet again, this time from Miss Beryl's perspective, seeing the world through her eyes and delaying Sully's entrance until the second chapter. Result? The same exact problem. I was no happier being trapped in this old woman's thoughts and perceptions than I'd been in Sully's. What I needed, it seemed, was not *out* but out*side*. I wanted to look *at* my characters, not *through* them. Something like, well, the following:

> . . . a controversy had erupted on the editorial page of the *North Bath Weekly Journal* over whether the plural of Saber-tooth should be Sabertooths or Saberteeth. When the cheer-leaders led the spell cheer, how should it go? The principal said Saberteeth sounded elitist and silly and dental. The chair of the high school's English department disagreed, claiming this latest outrage was yet another symptom of the erosion of the English language, and he threatened to resign if he and his staff were expected to sanction tooths as the plural of tooth. Why not? the public librarian had asked in the next letter to the editor. Wasn't this, after all, the same English department that had sanctioned "antelopes" as the plural of "antelope"? . . .

Nevertheless, this new banner read GO SABERTOOTHS! TROUNCE SCHUYLER SPRINGS! and the men whose job it was to string the banner across the street were more concerned with it than with the old banner, which had become gray and tattered in the wind . . . . And so, as the new banner was being attended to . . . the old banner was allowed to lie stretched across the street in the slush. When the workers were satisfied that the new banner was secure and had climbed down from their ladders, one of them picked up one end of the old banner just as a car drove by and hooked the cord with one of its rear wheels, dragging the banner all the way up Main and finally out of sight. Sully, shoveling Miss Beryl's driveway as promised, looked up and saw the banner trail by, though he had no idea what it was.

The freedom to move around from one character to another and to enter their thoughts at will, as well as the freedom to reveal what they know *(Bob kissed Ellen, but he was thinking of Sue, and Ellen was thinking of Tom)*, turns out to be just one of omniscience's many benefits. What the passage above illustrates is that it can also provide freedom *from* your characters. Neither Sully nor Miss Beryl is privy to the banner controversy as it plays out in the newspaper, which means I was under no obligation to view it through them. In other words, though your story is *about* your characters, there may be times when their presence is actually a hindrance, counterintuitive though that may seem. Further, while there's an obvious advantage to having easy access to what your characters know, what they don't grasp can be entertaining as well. When he looks up, Sully sees the banner go by, but he doesn't know what it is. The reader is ahead of him in terms of knowledge, not behind. And this, *precisely*, is what I'd been hoping for: a way of demonstrating that Sully's conclusions didn't always align with my own.

Here's the deal: when you *want* out, *get* out. Out is where omniscience lives, in part because being outside or apart from a writer's characters is a powerful incentive for him to locate his authorial voice, which is different from a voice he discovers by inventing a character like Nick Carraway or Holden Caulfield to speak for him. Holden may be sensitive and bright, but he's just a kid, with a kid's vocabulary, and while his voice might be an imaginative triumph, it's not the voice of the adult Salinger, even though the author is its ultimate source. By contrast, an autho-rial voice is one that exists entirely independent of any of the story's characters, while it's just as distinct and easy to describe as a fictional character's. When we first meet Dodger Hicks, he isn't "awaiting" a friend; he's "lying in wait" for one. Friend-ship by ambush. Grandfather's delusions are dispelled by "fresh blood . . . making a swing through his brain." The man whose legs are severed loses a lot of blood, but how many writers would choose to describe that loss as "lavish"? With every choice of word and phrase, Hassler is creating a portrait of the person tell-ing us the story, a self-portrait, really, one that must remain con-sistent (not earnest in one paragraph and sarcastic in the next). The authorial voice I adopted in *Nobody's Fool* is playful and wry. The principal of the high school objects to "Saberteeth" as "elit-ist and silly and dental." The reader kind of expects the first two adjectives, but "dental" makes the principal look like a fool. Of *course* teeth are dental. Then the chair of the English department pompously refuses to accept "tooths" as the plural of "tooth," despite having for decades accepted "antelopes" as the plural of "antelope," thus revealing himself to be a different kind of fool. Naturally, not a few readers will also have forgotten that the plu-ral here is actually "antelope," which means the joke's also on *them*. Is the authorial voice suggesting we're all fools? Why, yes. Are we supposed to lose sleep over that? Feel insulted? Appar-ently not, the condition of foolishness having been defined as pretty universal. But defined by whom? Well, *me*! See me, lurking over there in the rhetorical woods, waving to you, the guy with the big, goofy grin? And behind me, milling about among those same trees, are some ghosts. Most you won't recognize because they're members of my family, like my maternal grandfather, who was also wry and playful. ("Bingo used to be the bestus," he crooned to me as a child, in reference to Bing Crosby, whose career had taken a nosedive. "Now he's just like all the restus.") But some of the other shades are identifiable. That's Twain over there with the cloud of hair, and Dickens, because I hear them in my head, just as I hear my grandfather. As Whitman said: "I contain multitudes."

Given its obvious advantages, why then do so many writers, novice and experienced alike, instinctively shy away from omniscience? Here are a few of the objections I used to hear back in my teaching days.

1. *Omniscience stresses story*telling, *not showing,* and as such it runs contrary to the most famous of all writing maxims: *Show, don't tell.* Okay, but remember that we're called storytellers, not story*showers,* and the injunction against telling is aimed primarily at beginners, who are prone to summary. "Showing" forces the writer to slow down, to make use of the senses, to not be content skimming the narrative surface. All well and good, but the best writing is actually a blend of showing and telling. There's also the matter of cultural and historical context. Fifty years ago, if you wanted to be a writer it was probably because you loved to read books. These days many people who want to be writers come to storytelling through TV and movies and even video games. When you write for a screen, everything must be shown, because the only information a physical camera can convey is the physical world of the present moment.

What a character's thinking must be manifest in what he says and does. There's no such law in novel writing. It's also important to remember that telling the reader things can be a test of what the novice writer himself actually knows (or doesn't). The more limited (and limiting) points of view can offer the writer an attractive (yet dangerous) refuge from ignorance. If you know little about a subject, it's tempting to tell the story from the perspective of a character who's equally ignorant. You can blame your stupidity on him should the need arise. Omniscience offers great freedom that trails great responsibility.

2. *Omniscience feels old-fashioned.* Well, gentle reader, who gives a damn? Are we talking old-fashioned in the sense of belonging to a rich, extended literary tradition? There are worse things. Trendiness, for example.

3. *Omniscience is an arrogant technique.* For the moment, let's pretend that's true, that it's somehow immodest. Where is it written that writers are supposed to be meek? If playing God scares you, there are other professions. But in truth I seriously doubt the arrogance of omniscience. There's been a lot of chatter lately about cultural appropriation. Who has the right to speak for whom? For instance, what right do I, as a sixty-seven-year-old white American male, have to speak for a sixteen-year-old black girl living in Nigeria? On one side of the argument are those who claim the primacy of the literary imagination. Were it not for this, they argue, no writer would be permitted outside the boundaries of his or her own experience. The other side expresses frustration with the kind of colonization that occurs when well-off white writers tackle material that's far outside their realm

of personal experience and in the process drown out more authentic voices. How is that *not* privilege manifesting itself as arrogance? Okay, but the point of view one chooses to tell the story of the sixteen-year-old Nigerian girl is not irrelevant here, and omniscience, viewed in this light, may actually be *less* arrogant than, say, first person literary. Omniscience claims, in essence, *I'm going to tell you a story about a sixteen-year-old black girl who lives in Nigeria.* The reader's response to that may well be cautious: *Really? Do you know enough about sixteen-year-old black girls to pull that off? For that matter, do you know enough about Nigeria?* Some readers might think me foolhardy to undertake such a daunting task, but few would say I had no right to. But what about a more limited (more modest?) first-person point of view? What if I become just *one* person, the way actors are said to become their characters? (Paul Newman *is* Hud, the old movie poster proclaimed.) The problem inherent in such *becoming* is immediately apparent. When I maintain that I *am* Redeem, a sixteen-year-old Nigerian girl, everybody who knows better responds, *The fuck you are.* Moreover, every perceived mistake I make as Redeem will be met with resentment and derision. I'm not saying that omniscience resolves the dispute over cultural appropriation, only that when narrative problems have technical remedies, those remedies should not be ignored.

4. *Omniscient narrators are just an excuse for authorial intrusion.* Conventional wisdom does in fact dictate that it's not wise for a writer to insert himself into his story, and it's not bad advice, especially for beginners. And yet. Here's John Steinbeck, from *Cannery Row:*

What Frogs Think: A Defense of Omniscience

During the millennia that frogs and men have lived in the same world, it's probable that men have hunted frogs. And during that time a pattern of hunt and parry has developed. The man with net or bow or lance or gun creeps noiselessly, as he thinks, toward the frog. The pattern requires the frog to sit still, sit very still and wait. The rules of the game require the frog to wait until the final flicker of a second, when the net is descending, when the lance is in the air, when the finger squeezes the trigger, then the frog jumps, plops into the water, swims to the bottom and waits until the man goes away. That is the way it is done, the way it has always been done. Frogs have every right to expect it will always be done that way. Now and then the net is too quick, the lance pierces, the gun flicks and the frog is gone, but it is all fair and in the framework. Frogs don't resent that.

Not content to speak for all mankind, Steinbeck wants to speak for frogs as well. Any objections? PETA? The ASPCA? Anybody?

Probably the real reason apprentice writers shy away from omniscience is that they suspect they're not ready for it yet, and in this they may be right. Being drawn to omniscience has something to do with years in service, with experience of life, with the gradual accumulation of knowledge and pain and maybe even a little wisdom. As we mature we see patterns, and those can resolve themselves into worlds. We want to tell readers how those worlds (as well as the real one they're based on) work. At twenty-five or thirty, not many writers are anxious to assume so much responsibility. Omniscience entails not just the permission to speak but to speak with a kind of authority we know deep down hasn't really been granted, though we proceed as if it had, as if we actually do know everything we need to about the world, as if we really did, in godly fashion, invent the damn thing. It's an authority we seize, like riches, and accept, like grace, because omniscience is such a sweet, lovely, rewarding, generous stick shift of a technique, and it'll take you places you can't get to with an automatic transmission. The first few times you try it, it'll buck you all over the narrative road and send you fleeing back to those other vehicles you've already mastered, wondering why anybody would want to make an already difficult job that much harder. But if you're like me, you'll eventually return, not because omniscience is always the right way to tell a story but because, when it is, nothing else will do. Sometimes you just need to explain how frogs think.

Mark Twain's Nonfiction

The novelist William Dean Howells once famously remarked that his friend Mark Twain was not a writer who performed so much as a performer who wrote. Perhaps surprisingly, this astute observation also holds true in Twain's nonfiction, a form that would seem to put less of a premium on both invention and performance. To read *The Innocents Abroad, Roughing It, A Tramp Abroad* and *Life on the Mississippi* is to understand that Twain didn't lose much sleep over the idiosyncratic demands of fiction versus nonfiction. Both offered numerous and varied opportunities to an inspired, indeed unparalleled, bullshitter. Classifying Twain's work into fiction or nonfiction is something we do for our own convenience; *his* convenience was to ignore ours.

So, are the events chronicled in *Roughing It*—which details Twain's journey by stagecoach to the Nevada Territory, his stint there as a silver miner and his apprenticeship to the newspaper trade—true? Once asked that same question about one of his own stories, David Sedaris replied, "They're true enough," and it's easy to imagine Twain saying the same thing about his youthful adventures in the American West. We know he traveled to Europe and the Holy Land as a correspondent, so it's not unreasonable to suppose that at least some of what he reports in *The Innocents Abroad* actually happened. I suspect, however, that the literally true parts are those he wasn't able to improve on through embellishment or outright invention. For Twain, "truth" was not just elastic but indeed designed to be stretched. He learned this lesson early on, writing for western newspapers. He explains the job to great comic effect in *Roughing It*, where, as a cub reporter, he wrote a story about a wagon full of immigrants attacked by Indians. At first, fearing that other reporters might recount the same story, he sticks pretty close to the facts, despite his conviction that the story could be improved upon by straying from them. Later, though, when he learns that the owner of the wagon meant to continue his journey the following morning (leaving no one to contradict Twain's account), all bets are off. His next draft describes an Indian fight that "to this day has no parallel in history." This is Twain we're talking about, so it's likely that he also exaggerated the extent of his exaggerations, but still. Buoyed by praise from the paper's editor, he expresses a willingness to murder every immigrant on the plains with his pen if "the interests of the paper demanded it." Thus the low bar of truth is established: true enough. For him. For his editor. For the paper's readership.

His approach to fiction was basically the same. At the beginning of the *Adventures of Huckleberry Finn*, Huck says that readers may have heard of him if they've read *The Adventures of Tom Sawyer*, which "was made by Mr. Mark Twain, and he told the truth, mainly. There was things which he stretched, but mainly he told the truth." That first assertion, it's worth remembering, was both the truth and a lie. The book was actually "made" by Samuel Clemens, and the parts Mr. Clemens "stretched" were the parts that needed stretching, beginning with his own identity as Mark Twain. Again, Twain is not so much a writer, at least as the term is used today, as a storyteller whose primary duties are to the narrative and its audience. No story is likely to be instructive if it isn't entertaining, and the best way to gauge whether it's working or not is to watch it land with an actual audience, a lesson Twain learned long before he gave his first public lecture.

In *A Tramp Abroad* he recounts his first ride on a Mississippi steamboat as a ten-year-old boy. Falling asleep, he has a terrifying dream that the boat is ablaze, and he rushes into the ladies' salon, still under the nightmare's influence, screaming "Fire!" The ladies there knew better, of course, and they advised him to return to his cabin and dress, lest he catch cold. It's a revealing memory. The humiliation of his story playing so badly, his audience rejecting both the tale and the teller, is still fresh in Twain's mind twenty-five years later as he's writing *Tramp*. Just as telling is the reason he recalls the episode in the first place. He's in Germany watching a production of *King Lear*, where the actor playing the title role "raged and wept and howled" across the stage. Twain admires the performance but feels sorry for the actor, who has to wait until the end of the act for his applause.

Writers, by contrast, are used to silence. Their applause, if they're lucky enough to get any, comes long after their "performance" has concluded, in the form of reviews. True, authors who publish serially may to some degree interact with their audience. When readers loved Sam Weller in an early installment of *The Pickwick Papers*, Dickens was happy to expand his role as the novel progressed, but that's hardly akin to telling the same stories onstage night after night, as Twain did on his public-speaking tours. Each audience provided him with valuable insight into what worked and why, allowing him to revise the material accordingly. His first public lecture triumph near the end of *Roughing It* is described almost completely in terms of the crowd's appreciation. The audience is with him from the start, he tells us, even the jokes he'd judged to be inferior faring "royally." Near the end, though, the material grows more somber and serious, and Twain tells us that the "absorbed hush" that fell over the audience "gratified me more than any applause." Indeed, he's so pleased by the reaction that he can't help but smile, which the crowd took as a cue to laugh, thus ruining the moment.

Later in life, Twain's relationship with his audience would grow more complex. In *Life on the Mississippi*, he admits that being a river pilot was the best job he ever had, because the steamboat pilot has no master, whereas writers were "manacled servants of the public." That said, no writer ever courted his audience more assiduously nor drew more confidence and pleasure from public adulation. (Twain courted honorary degrees, too, and shamelessly.) Indeed, one suspects that it was from his audience, as much as the work itself, that Twain derived his sense of accomplishment and well-being.

It's worth pointing out that the world has changed since Twain left it, and our attitudes toward "truth" and "fiction" have become more rigorous and stern. Mislabel your novel as a memoir (or allow your publisher to do so) and you'll likely find yourself in a world of hurt. Twain was no great fan of fraud and deception, but like Melville he understood that the world was steeped in both, and moreover he harbored more than a little admiration and affection for its charlatans. Reading *Huckleberry Finn* I often wonder if I judge the King and the Duke more harshly than their creator intended. At the very least Twain would've understood that people who get conned are often complicit in their own deception. Just as important, he would have recognized the paradox inherent in labeling some stories "made up" (fiction) and others "true" (nonfiction). Interestingly, audience often plays a role here, too. When you claim that a story is invented—especially one as elaborate as Twain's were—people will naturally suspect you of telling the truth *(Come on! You couldn't have made that up!)*. Conversely, when you claim to be telling the truth, those same folks shift gears and suspect you of lying *(Surely you embellished this!)*. Storytelling thrives in this fundamental paradox and often resists any attempts at clarification.

The world has changed in other ways, too, since Twain's departure. Seen in proper historical context, he appears in so many respects—in his embrace of technology, his use of the vernacular, his attitudes toward race, colonialism and, later, the abomination of slavery—forward-thinking, a man ahead of his time. However, though it pains me to say this, there is, by contemporary standards, some pretty cringe-worthy stuff in these pages. In *The Innocents Abroad,* observing the two men in a Paris parade, Twain sees in Emperor Napoleon III "the representative of the highest modern civilization, progress, and refinement," whereas the Turkish sultan Abdul Aziz, sized up from a distance as "stupid" and "unprepossessing," represents a people "filthy, brutish, ignorant, unprogressive, [and] superstitious." In Palestine, Twain's party comes upon a group of homeless, impoverished people by the side of the road. Among them are a mother and child; from afar, it looks like the child is wearing goggles, but up close they see that its eyes are infested with flies which the mother can't be bothered to shoo away. Twain notes how this "usual assemblage of squalid humanity . . . sat in silence, and with tireless patience watched our every motion with that vile, uncomplaining impoliteness which is so truly Indian and which makes a white man so nervous and uncomfortable and savage that he wants to exterminate the whole tribe." Yikes.

Closer to home in *Roughing It*, he describes the western coyote as having a "blood kinship" with the American Indian, both of which will "eat anything they can bite." The "Goshoot" tribe of the Nevada Territory is a "silent, sneaking, treacherous looking race . . . always hungry, and yet never refusing anything that a hog would eat, though often eating what a hog would decline." From our privileged twenty-first-century vantage point, we can't help wishing our nineteenth-century literary hero would identify what he's witnessing as poverty and ignorance, not innate depravity. And female readers will surely note that women don't seem to register fully on Twain's consciousness and imagination. Nor do the poor and downtrodden always elicit the sympathy we might expect. Twain describes Parisian slum dwellers as "savage-looking ruffians" who "take as much genuine pleasure in building a barricade as they do in cutting a throat or shoving a friend into the Seine." Nor, at times, is he above playing the least fortunate for laughs: "If you want dwarfs—I mean just a few dwarfs for a curiosity—go to Genoa. If you wish to buy them by the gross, for retail, go to Milan . . . the crop [is] luxuriant." But if Twain was a man of his time and not ours, it's also worth noting that his convictions evolved during his life. For instance, throughout *The Innocents Abroad*, he identifies himself as a Christian and as such compares himself and his fellow pilgrims favorably with non-Christians and pagans, who are typically depicted as superstitious, cruel and violence prone. But in *The Mysterious Stranger* fragments, which were among the last things he wrote, he has the angel Satan tell the story's protagonist that "two or three centuries from now it will be recognized that all the competent killers are Christians." And who is to blame? Why, the Christian God, "who could make good children as easily as bad, yet preferred to make bad ones."

More often, though, he is our Mark Twain, compassionate, broad-minded and fatherly, more the man we've come to expect from reading *Huckleberry Finn* and *Pudd'nhead Wilson,* whose moral register we can admire. In *Roughing It,* he considers as purest bigotry the shabby treatment of the Chinese, who were essential to both the building of the transcontinental railroad and the settlement of the West: "They are a harmless race when white men either let them alone or treat them no worse than dogs . . . A disorderly Chinaman is rare, and a lazy one does not exist." On their behalf he demands fairness, justice. "Any white man can swear a Chinaman's life away in the courts, but no Chinaman can testify against a white man." And once aroused, his sympathies are both righteous and fierce. "Only the scum of the population" abuse the Chinese, he asserts, they and "policemen and politicians . . . the dust-licking pimps and slaves of the scum." With very few exceptions he can be counted on to take the side of the oppressed over the oppressor. In *The Innocents Abroad,* the prisoner consigned for political reasons to the dungeons of the Doge's palace in Venice lives "without light, air, books; naked, unshaven, uncombed, covered with vermin; his useless tongue forgetting its office, with none to speak to."

And his heart goes out to all abused animals, even to the notorious, much-maligned dogs of Constantinople: "I never saw such utterly wretched, starving, sad-visaged, broken-hearted-looking curs in my life." "Do I contradict myself?" Walt Whitman asked in "Song of Myself," before immediately answering in the affirmative. If Twain embodies his own fair share of contradictions, we do well to remember that he too was "large" and "contained multitudes."

Of course the prevailing characteristic of Twain's storytelling is his witty, playful exuberance. He loves to tell us one thing while showing us another, ascribing, for instance, a laudable, benevolent motive to a human behavior when a baser one is actually on display. Again in Palestine, fearing an attack by Bedouins, he tells us, "My first impulse was to dash forward and destroy [them] . . . My second was to dash to the rear to see if there were any coming in that direction. I acted on the latter impulse. So did all the others. If any Bedouins had approached us, then, from that point on the compass, they would have paid dearly for their rashness." Taking painting lessons in *A Tramp Abroad*, he tells us, tongue firmly implanted in cheek, that he's been complimented by his teachers for having "a manner of my own . . . that if I ever painted the commonest type of a dog, I should be sure to throw a something into the aspect of that dog which would keep him from being mistaken for the creation of any other artist," and after many months of arduous study, his German is described by one of his teachers as "very rare, possibly 'unique.'" By the end of his life Twain would rail against the "damned human race," but in these pages we see a writer still buoyant and hopeful enough to regard human foolishness as grand entertainment, and far from exempting himself from folly, he's all too willing (as above) to make himself the butt of the joke. If others are fools and hypocrites, well, they have him (and, if we're honest, us) for company. In Gibraltar he buys a pair of kid gloves that are manifestly too small, tearing them to shreds as he tugs them on and off, all because the merchant keeps complimenting him on how perfect they look on him. Elsewhere he tells the story of a tiresome, grouchy fellow who keeps banging on about how perfectly wretched the coffee has been during their travels, offering as evidence the pale, transparent liquid he happens just then to be drinking. Taking a taste, his companion admits that as coffee it leaves a great deal to be desired, but that it's tolerably good tea. Only at the anecdote's conclusion does Twain identify the chastened fool as himself.

Such passages, together with unforgettable set pieces on shaving, dueling, profanity, singing gondoliers, Turkish baths and the ridiculous German language, make apparent just how much *fun* Twain had writing. I mention this because not every writer does have fun, and not all who do are willing to admit it. For Twain, much of the sheer joy of storytelling is language itself. All good writers take pleasure in locating the precise right word for the occasion. Twain, who in a letter to William Dean Howells called a man "a quadrilateral, astronomical, incandescent son of a bitch," finds equal delight in locating the perfect wrong one. In order to tell the story of his grandfather's ram, it's necessary for the storyteller, Jim Blaine, to become "tranquilly, serenely, *symmetrically* drunk" (my emphasis), and in real life Twain takes particular delight in people like Mr. Ballou, also in *Roughing It,* who loves the *sound* of words, irrespective of their meaning and context. His ire up, he accuses a man named Ollendorff of being dumber than a "logarithm." That gentleman, deeply wounded, later admits he has no idea what the word means except that it's obviously "a thing considered disgraceful and unbecoming in America." When young Sam didn't learn the Mississippi River fast enough to suit his "gunpowdery" teacher and mentor, Mr. Bixby, the man "went off with a bang . . . and then went on loading and firing until he was out of adjectives." Twain himself never runs out of them. He describes a riverboat captain named Brown as a "middle-aged, long, slim, bony, smooth-shaven, horse-faced, ignorant, stingy, malicious, snarling, fault-hunting, mote-magnifying tyrant." Who says, *Show, don't tell?* In addition to words, Twain is deeply devoted to every sort of comic illogic and fallacy. "There is probably no pleasure equal to the pleasure of climbing a dangerous Alp; but it is a pleasure which is confined strictly to people who can find pleasure in it." His inability to *keep* promises, he explains (lest it be considered a character flaw), is the quite natural and understandable result of his too-large and generous capacity to *make* them. "The surest way to stop writing about Rome," he informs us, as if we'll all have need of this advice one day, "is to stop."

Also on display throughout these pages is Twain the iconoclast, who has little use for received wisdom. Prone to invention and embellishment himself, he's naturally suspicious of the authority of others. Taking in the sights of Europe, he steadfastly refuses to allow professional guides (and, especially, guidebooks) to trump the evidence of his own senses. Those who revere "the old masters" for their "sublimity," "feeling" and "richness of coloring" come under sharp, unrelenting attack. "I envy them their honest admiration, if it be honest—their delight, if they feel delight . . . But at the same time the thought *will* intrude itself upon me, How can they see what is not visible? . . . What would you think of a man who stared in ecstasy upon a desert of stumps and said: 'Oh . . . what a noble forest is here!'" German opera? Twain finds it insufferable, though he has a theory as to its popularity across the Atlantic. Opera's ingenuity, he argues, is that "it deals so largely in pain that its scattered delights are prodigiously augmented by the contrasts . . . just as an honest man in politics shines more than he would elsewhere." He has little doubt that one day Americans will like opera, too: "One in fifty" already does, the other forty-nine attending "in order to learn to like it, and the rest in order to be able to talk knowingly about it." They hum along "so that their neighbors may perceive that they have been to operas before. The funerals of these do not occur often enough."

What's most thrilling to witness here is the emergence of Twain's voice, which he seems to have invented not just for himself but for the young nation he clearly feels at liberty to speak for. That voice, its distinctive attitude and posture, has become so much a part of us that it's hard to remember there was ever a time when there was simply nothing like it. Its unexpected freshness, like the emergence, later, of jazz or rock and roll, was actually part of its message. In *The Innocents Abroad* and *A Tramp Abroad* he puts Europe and the rest of the world under the microscope, but the lens he peers through is strictly American, meaning that he has as much to say about us, the viewers, as the viewed. It's the American character—our energy, practicality, arrogance, competence, anti-intellectualism and congenital optimism—that thus emerges. His use of arithmetic to suggest the fraudulence of European relics (added up, there are enough nails and slivers of the true cross to make dozens of them, and there appear to be at least two complete sets of the

Apostle John's ashes) are hilarious enough in their own right, but they also make the case that America, a nation too young to have a past, really isn't missing much. At the castle in Heidelberg he buys for a pittance a painting of a duke and another of a princess so that he might start "a portrait gallery of my ancestors," remarking that "one can lay in ancestors at even cheaper rates than these." In Titian, Tintoretto, Raphael, Rubens and Veronese he sees men of "cringing spirit," toadies willing to genuflect before "such monsters as the French, Venetian, and Florentine Princes," something no American would do. Regarding the riches of the Vatican and "priest-ridden" Italy, he goes off (forgive me) like a Roman candle: "Raphael pictured such infernal villains as Catherine and Marie de Médicis seated in heaven and conversing familiarly with the Virgin Mary and the angels." "Alas! those good old times are gone," he says elsewhere, "when a murderer could wipe the stain from his name . . . by building an addition to a church."

When he's not busy mocking European snobbery and pretension, he's having fun playing with the stereotype of the parochial, self-satisfied American abroad. Seeing Notre Dame for the first time, he assures us, "We had heard of it before." Like Washington Irving before him, he often depicts his fellow pilgrims as slow-witted, a step behind (like Brom Bones), when in reality they're steps ahead. Throughout Europe they allow their guides—all of whom they call Ferguson, rather than learn to pronounce their names—to deliver long lectures about this or that Renaissance or medieval artist, only to inquire when Ferguson's voice finally falls, "Is he dead?"

And yet in the two books where America itself is put under the microscope—*Roughing It* and *Life on the Mississippi*—Twain displays both pride and profound misgivings about the American character that is surfacing. As in *Huckleberry Finn,* he regards violence as part of the nation's DNA. As a lover of tall tales, he immediately recognizes its inherent comic potential. On his first day in Carson City he witnesses a dispute between a man named Harris and another who had recently identified him as the robber of a stagecoach. The former "began to rebuke the stranger with a six-shooter, and the stranger began to explain with another." When both revolvers are empty, Harris, full of "picturesque" bullet holes, rides on with a "polite nod." Twain's depiction of the fearsome outlaw Slade is similarly cartoonish. Real violence, which Twain equates with cruelty, is different, and he evinces little taste or stomach for either. He discovers early that there's nothing romantic about death. Sneaking home late one night he finds a corpse in his father's office: "A white human hand lay in the moonlight! Such an awful sinking at the heart—such a sudden gasp for breath! I felt—I can not tell what I felt." With cartoon violence, his instinct is to embellish; with real violence (in life or violence made real in fiction), he instead draws the curtain, as at the end of the Grangerford-Shepherdson feud in *Huckleberry Finn,* where Huck explains that he won't be telling us about all the things he witnessed because "it would make me sick again." In *Life on the Mississippi,* Twain is similarly reticent in describing the death of his brother Henry after a steamboat explosion. "On the evening of the sixth day his wandering mind busied itself with matters far away . . . His hour had struck; we bore him to the death-room, poor boy." What's fascinating about his lengthy account of the explosion's aftermath is that most of Twain's attention is devoted not to his brother at all but rather to the boat's chief mate, whose horrific injuries are described in harrowing detail. Three times the man is carried to the death room, only to rally there and curse his attendant. Why focus on the mate instead of his own brother? Because the mate "lived to be mate of a steamboat again." Life trumps death—it's that simple.

Is such optimism a matter of youth? Faith? If the latter, faith in what? God? Perhaps, sometimes. In these early books, though he gleefully skewers conformist piety, Twain shows both respect and admiration for genuine faith, like that of the Dominican fathers who minister to the sick and dying during the plague. More often, though, his faith seems to reside in the seemingly incorruptible spirit and innocence of individuals like Tom and Huck, the unflagging devotion and love radiating from men like Jim. We sense that it's because of them he can believe in his fledgling nation, in the progress it represents. At the end of *Life on the Mississippi* he returns to Hannibal and locates the house he grew up in before he, like Huck, lit out for the territories. "The people who now occupy it are of no more value than I am; but in my time they would have been worth not less than five hundred dollars apiece. They are colored folk."

Should it trouble us that in the end Twain's optimism was unsustainable? Maybe. Should it surprise us? Probably not. If despair isn't a potent source of comedy—and many argue that it is—it's all too often the fate of the comic artist. There comes a day when all that you've managed to keep at bay through humor just isn't funny anymore, which may be why comic geniuses often do their best work early. G. K. Chesterton preferred Dickens's first novel, *The Pickwick Papers*, to all that followed. Not many would agree with that assessment, but there is much to be said for the novels that preceded *Bleak House*, their sheer delight in the world, their author's youthful chutzpah. The Mark Twain of these early- to midcareer books clearly felt equal to whatever task was put before him. Sure, even as a young man he was acquainted with loss and failure, but these had not yet begun to take their toll, which is another way of saying he'd not yet really begun to internalize them. That would come later.

Meanwhile, he was, like the nation he spoke for, confident, irreverent, exuberant, unapologetic, full of swagger, untroubled by self-doubt and, perhaps most important, dead game. A force of nature. Something new in the world.

The Boss in Bulgaria

I almost didn't make the trip. My Boston flight was delayed and then delayed further and finally canceled altogether. Like so many overseas flights these days, this one was full, which meant that hundreds of passengers would have to be accommodated on other flights, and since ours was one of the last scheduled out of International Terminal E, that wouldn't happen until morning. If I conceded defeat right then, I might catch the last bus back to Portland, Maine, where I lived. Whereas if I joined my fellow passengers at the thinly staffed customer-service counter, that sensible option would vanish, and I'd be stuck in Boston overnight. Worse, even if I was lucky enough to snag an early morning flight to Frankfurt, I would've already missed my connecting flight to Bulgaria. There wouldn't be another until the following day, and there was no guarantee I'd get a seat. Worst-case scenario, I'd be stranded in the Frankfurt airport without my luggage, unable to get to Bulgaria and, if flights back to Boston were full, powerless to return home for who knew how long. Why run that risk?

I had a cell-phone number for Elizabeth Kostova, whose foundation organized the annual conference I was attending. The problem was that she and many of her colleagues and the other American writers, all departing from other cities, would already be in the air, so in fact there was no one from whom I could get advice, though, to be honest, it wasn't really advice I was after so much as permission to bail. Because this Bulgaria writers' conference fit rather snugly into the category of "good deeds," didn't it? Sure, I was being paid, but the real reason I'd agreed to participate was my fondness for Elizabeth, a writer whose books I admired. Each year her foundation brought together a contingent of American and British authors with Bulgarian ones in the hopes of encouraging, after decades of communism, their own national literature. Good, necessary work. On the other hand, what did I have to do with Bulgaria or it with me? Such self-serving questions generally don't occur to you when things are going smoothly, only when they unexpectedly pivot and head due south, when what was supposed to be easy suddenly becomes difficult. Standing there with my haggard fellow travelers and feeling like a bait-and-switch victim, I wanted out, so I looked in the folder containing my travel instructions and contact phone numbers and found one—for a foundation staff person with whom I'd been corresponding—that wasn't a cell phone. Maybe I'd be able to reach someone there. It was too late to make such a call, but if the person I was trying to reach was already on a flight, I rationalized, no one would pick up, right? I could leave my message—*Flight canceled. No good options. Sorry. I tried my best*—and hang up, inconveniencing no one. Imagine my chagrin, then, when a sleepy-sounding man with a thick accent answered on the second ring. When I identified myself, he seemed to know who I was. "Yes! Yes!" he said.

"My flight's been canceled," I told him. "It doesn't look like I'm going to be able to make it. I'm sorry."

"But, you . . ." he said, pausing to locate the right expression in English. "You are the star!"

My impulse was to deny this, to tell him there were several excellent writers on the trip, and that of course the real star was Elizabeth herself. But I knew what he meant. Yes, this was her conference, but *she* participated every year. This year, like it or not, mine was the marquee name. Since winning the Pulitzer a decade earlier, I'd become increasingly ambivalent about celebrity, an attitude I probably wasn't entitled to. After all, wasn't fame simply a by-product of what I'd worked so hard to achieve for so long? Add to that the fact that the message I intended to leave—*I tried my best*—wasn't really true, was it? "Okay," I told him. "I'll see what I can do."

Well, shit, I thought, hanging up and noting the time. There was a good chance I'd already missed that last bus to Portland. Apparently I was going to Bulgaria. Or at least to Frankfurt. There were still about seventy-five people ahead of me in the customer-service line. The man at the front had been talking to the lone agent for the last fifteen minutes. Nothing to do but hunker down. At some point I realized that an old Moody Blues song I'd heard on the radio earlier in the day was running through my brain. Dear Lord, when was the last time I'd thought of them? In the run-up to this conference I'd been sent a questionnaire by the producer of a television talk show on which I was to appear. They had a copy of my most recent book but wanted background information on its author. Who and what were my cultural influences? Could I list some of my favorite books, artists, musicians? I'd mentioned Dickens and Twain, Edward Hopper, and Springsteen, of course. Though I'd liked them well enough as an undergraduate back in the seventies, there were probably five hundred bands I would've listed before the Moody Blues, but it was their lyric that was now running through my head on a loop: "I'm just a singer in a rock and roll band . . . I'm just a singer in . . ."

Except I wasn't. Assuming I got to Bulgaria, I would be a literary rock star of sorts for the next week. Home. My own bed. Work. These were what I wanted. What I always wanted.

The annual conference was a big deal there. Its serious work—a week's worth of workshops, lectures and individual conferences—took place in Sozopol, a resort town on the Black Sea, but for publicity reasons it always began and ended in Sofia, the capital. Thanks to my travel delays I'd missed both the orientation activities and the first full day of the conference. Now we were off to Sozopol, a five-hour bus ride.

My seatmate was the well-known biographer Elizabeth Frank, who'd done the conference before and could help me interpret what I was seeing out the windows. I'd been surprised by how vibrant Sofia was, its cafés and coffee shops full of young people flush with freedom and hope after the fall of communism. In the countryside, Liz explained, things were very different. Out here, many people remembered communism fondly. Maybe there'd been no food in the markets, maybe there were times when it seemed like everyone might starve, but at least back then all and sundry were in the same boat. Now the stores were full of food, but it was unaffordable, so how, they wondered, was this better? While some of the Bulgarian countryside looked well tended and prosperous, especially the vineyards, there were also long stretches of fallow, weedy poverty. According to Liz, what prosperity there was came from outside, EU money streaming in and buying up everything on the cheap. Asked how such a thing could happen, the old-timers had a ready explanation: *It's the Jews.* "Seriously?" I said. "*This* again?" "Right," Liz sighed. "This again."

At some point our conversation turned more personal, and Liz told me a story that I would think about often in the days to come. When she was a little girl, living with her family in New York City, she was sometimes awakened late at night by loud voices. One was her father's; the other belonged to his writing partner. They were TV comedy writers and what they were arguing over so passionately was whether a line from this week's show *was* or *was not* funny. To Liz, getting woke up by their ardent bickering was both comforting and inspiring. If good writing was worth arguing over, like politics, it must be important. Maybe she'd be a writer herself one day.

Hearing this story left me feeling strangely bereft, because as a kid I, too, had been awakened in the middle of the night by loud voices, my mother telling my father to keep his voice down, because their son was asleep in the next room. *What is wrong with you,* she always wanted to know. And his response: *Okay, Jean, how about you just kiss my ass?* And then one day all that stopped because he was gone. Years later, when I told him I wanted to be a writer, he didn't try to discourage me, though to him it was clearly a puzzling ambition. But it must've seemed as natural to Liz's dad as it later did to Liz herself that she would become a writer. He was, she told me, her first mentor, and for the rest of his life he remained one of her most faithful readers and champions. My own father would die before my first novel was published, leaving me to wonder, with each new book, what he would've made of it all.

In Sozopol we writers took over a small hotel built on a bluff overlooking the Black Sea. To get to the beach, you had to wind down through narrow one-way streets. Across the bay several modern condo developments had sprung up, and others were being built—more EU money—and this new construction offered a startling contrast to the quaint, almost fairy-tale architecture of the old town. Everywhere you looked, you saw the confluence of cultures—nearby Greece, Turkey, the former Soviet bloc. I found myself wondering what in all this, after centuries of conquest and subjugation, was actually Bulgarian?

The teaching was challenging. Many of the Bulgarians spoke some English, though for the most part we communicated through translators. Mornings, the Bulgarian- and English-speaking faculty and fellows had separate writing workshops, but in the afternoon the lectures and panels were translated, Bulgarian into English and vice versa, and at meals every effort was made to combine the groups, in part so the food, mysterious to us foreigners, could be explained. ("Really? You're supposed to eat these tiny deep-fried fish head and all?") The Bulgarians were all singers and serious drinkers, and after dinner they congregated on the hotel patio for long nights of song and cheap red wine. (I'd forgotten how much of the brutal, hangover-inducing wine we'd drunk as graduate students—back when I was just a singer in a rock and roll band—came from Bulgaria.) Not wanting to be unsociable, we Americans and Brits would join in for a while, but we had our morning workshops and afternoon talks to prepare, so one by one we drifted away. My room was on the third floor, its balcony overlooking the patio below, and I was awakened several times each night by singing that became more boisterous as the hours lengthened. Bulgarian folk songs came first, though at some point those segued into American rock and pop. There seemed to be a special fondness for Bon Jovi, and that first night, when I heard them bellowing "Oh! We're halfway there. Oh-oh, livin' on a prayer," I went out onto the balcony and peered down into the dark, thinking a few Americans and Brits had rejoined them, but no, the singers were all Bulgarian.

Was that how it seemed to them, one brief generation after the fall of communism? That they were halfway there? And how they felt as artists searching for their voices after decades of enforced silence? Did the Anglo-American presence contribute to their buoyant optimism? One thing was for sure: none of the singers in the courtyard below had ever been woken in the middle of the night by a parent arguing over whether something was funny or not. I suspected their fathers were more like mine than Liz Frank's. While they wouldn't want to stand in the way of their children's dreams, neither would they comprehend why, with so many needful things in the world, their kids would want to tell stories, write poems, paint pictures.

Near the end of his life, battling Alzheimer's, the novelist Ross Macdonald wrote to Eudora Welty, "I think you may understand . . . how hard it can be to speak after a lapse into silence."

Indeed. The human voice, like any other instrument, needs to be used. What do you say if you haven't spoken all day? All week? All year? What if you haven't been allowed a voice your entire life? What if the same was true of your parents, even your grandparents? Would everything you've been wanting to say for so long come gushing out? Probably not, actually. Or so it seemed of my Bulgarian writers, whose manuscripts I read in translation. Most of them were talented and, yes, anxious to enter the literary conversation from which they'd been excluded for so long. They wanted not only to write but also to start magazines and publishing houses for their stories and poems to appear in. They wanted all these things at once. But again, how? Do you go directly to the big subject—what life was like under totalitarian rule? If so, should that be treated as serious drama? As satire? Are you allowed to forget all that? Giddy with freedom, are you allowed to be happy? Devout? Sure, you're now free to say anything you want, but what should you say first? These seemed to be the unspoken questions lurking behind the Bulgarians' manuscripts. Or, to put it another way, how do you sing alone, on the page, in the light of day, like you do collectively, at night, at the edge of the Black Sea? Where do you find the confidence necessary to create a voice uniquely your own? Halfway there? Perhaps, but isn't it also possible that you're just beginning? And here's an even more alarming thought: *What if there's no you yet?* What if your writerly identity has to be invented before speech is possible?

How sweet and generous (and perhaps naïve?) it was of these Bulgarian writers to imagine we could help them. How intently they listened to us when we told them what we liked best about their stories and plays and essays, what we thought was working, and where their tone shifted unexpectedly, wrong-footing us. How good-naturedly they endured our probing personal questions: How did they feel about what they were reporting? What emotion motivated the telling? In a sense, coming from the other side of the world to advise a group of writers whose experiences of life were so different from my own seemed arrogant, but then again the problem of locating the right voice with which to speak is pretty universal. Black writers often feel the need to address their blackness, women writers their gender, gay writers their sexual orientation. No doubt they would all love the privilege blithely assumed by white male authors: the complete, unfettered freedom that derives from being unshackled from unfair expectations.

Yet as Melville's Ishmael once asked, "Who ain't a slave?" Even the most blessed writers encounter obstacles. We all shoulder burdens, even if they aren't equally heavy. Wouldn't it be wonderful, we can't help thinking, to simply set them down and walk away? Shouldn't that be an option? Consider a writer like Kenneth Millar, who grew up in Canada, moved to Southern California and there invented the aforementioned Ross Macdonald, who in turn invented Detective Lew Archer as well as the city of Santa Teresa (his fictional Santa Barbara). More than anything, it was Archer's tough, world-weary voice that anchored that brilliant series of detective novels. But to read Macdonald's dazzling correspondence with Eudora Welty in *Meanwhile There Are Letters* is to understand that while Archer's voice might be Macdonald's, it certainly isn't Millar's. Ken Millar was no wisecracking tough guy. The voice we hear in his letters to Welty is educated, intellectual, sensitive, at times almost effete—the quiet voice of the bird-watcher he was: indeed, it's the voice of a man whose experience of life could not have been further removed from that of his detective hero. Whatever Millar's burdens might have been, he seems to have set them down and walked away.

As a young writer I vividly remember trying to achieve just such a metamorphosis in my graduate writing program in Arizona, a place as far from my home in upstate New York as Millar's California was from his native Ontario. While I would have loved to write books like Macdonald's, and even tried my hand at detective stories, such a radical metamorphosis simply wasn't possible for me, so in the end I had little choice but to return, at least imaginatively, to my heart's home and be who I was, who I'd always been and, it appeared, I was meant to be. I had come to realize that I'd inherited a patch of dirt about the size of Faulkner's and had to figure out how to be content with that. At the time, though, my inability to invent a new, improved self felt like nothing so much as defeat.

But what of my Bulgarians? Who should *they* be? Should they embrace their burdens, as I did, or toss them off like shackles, as Millar was somehow able to do? This was what they seemed to want me to tell them: who they were, what they should value most, how to get from where they were to where I was. And so each night I carefully read their manuscripts, looking for clues to their identities. And every night, in the courtyard below, they sang, first the unknowable songs of their country, then the songs of my own. Night after night they insisted they're halfway there.

Back in Sofia, the conference winding down, I geared up for my TV appearance. One of the benefits of having been a teacher for so long, as well as a veteran of many book tours, is that I generally don't get nervous about public appearances, though I was a bit anxious with this one. It was live, not taped, and I was to be the last guest on the ninety-minute show, which meant that any anxiety I might be feeling would likely intensify as I watched the other guests from the wings. Naturally, I'd be working with yet another interpreter, and nothing is more lost in translation more quickly than humor, my strong suit. But never mind, I told myself. What happens in Bulgaria stays in Bulgaria.

The program was clearly modeled on American and British talk shows, its host an attractive woman who was seated at the center of a horseshoe-shaped piano bar. Her cohort—combining the duties of Ed McMahon and Doc Severinsen—was a young fellow at the piano, who would sometimes banter with the host but mostly just noodled at the keyboard as she talked with her guests, all of whom entered the studio—I kid you not—through a haze of dry-ice smoke.

When it was finally my turn, I climbed aboard the last remaining stool at the piano bar, and my translator nestled up close, whispering the host's first question in my ear, something about how it felt to win the Pulitzer Prize, and my heart leaped with gratitude. I knew the answer to *this* one! Not in Bulgarian, of course, but still. I'd been warned to keep my answers short, a challenge since I like long answers. They keep the next question, which you may not know the answer to, at bay. But guess what? I knew the answer to that one as well, so I gave it confidently, even risking a mild witticism, at which the host threw back her head and laughed, and the pianist did a comic little arpeggio on the keyboard. I was a hit! Evidently, even on the other side of the world I was a funny guy.

More questions. More answers. More noodling at the piano.

At some point, though, I became aware of movement in my peripheral vision and noticed the other guests glancing in the direction of whatever was going on behind me. Was it my imagination or had the noodling on the piano, atonal a moment earlier, begun to resolve itself into a melody, a tune I knew? What was it?

Stay focused, I told myself. My segment couldn't have more than three or four more minutes left. Apparently I was going to survive. Indeed, the host was now grinning like she was about to award me a second Pulitzer right there. *What was that damn tune?* "Well, Richard Russo," said the English voice in my ear, "we understand you're a fan of Bruce Springsteen, who is very popular here in Bulgaria, so this is our way of saying, 'Welcome to Sofia, and please do come again.'"

Rotating on my stool I saw there were now three more musicians—bassist, guitarist and drummer—and when they joined in I suddenly recognized the song. When the guitarist stepped up to the mic, I heard the lyric in my brain a split second before his voice reached my ear: *Grab your ticket and your suitcase, thunder's rollin' down this track. Well, you don't know where you're goin', now, but you know you won't be back. Well, darlin' if you're weary lay your head upon my chest. We'll take what we can carry, yeah, and we'll leave the rest.* The singer had a pretty good voice. Not like Bruce's, of course, but not bad either. What I couldn't tell was if the words were being sung phonetically, or if the singer actually understood them. *Oh, this train carries saints and sinners, this train carries losers and winners, this train carries whores and gamblers, this train carries lost souls.* Did the singer comprehend that he was singing a great American anthem, maybe the greatest written in my lifetime, by the greatest storytelling songwriter of his generation? Did he understand it was Springsteen's voice that had helped a weary nation through the bitter end of the Vietnam War, the AIDS epidemic, the attack on the World Trade Center? I couldn't tell, and somehow the possibility that he *didn't* know the meaning of those words caused my throat to constrict. *Well, big wheels roll through fields where sunlight streams. Oh, meet me in a land of hope and dreams.* Dear God, I thought. I'm about to break down sobbing on Bulgarian television. And if I do, it will *not* stay in Bulgaria. *I said this train, dreams will not be thwarted, this train, faith will be rewarded, this train, steel wheels singin', this train, bells of freedom ringin'.*

I will draw the curtain here, leaving it to the reader's imagination whether I maintained some semblance of dignity and decorum or wept like a child on the far side of the world, wept for pride in Bruce and the nation that spawned him, with a welling up of admiration, too, for every singer, poet and artist lucky enough to find, against all odds, a voice and the courage to raise it, and of deep empathy for the many more who try and fail. And yes, yes, profound admiration for my Bulgarians who sang and drank the night away in the conviction they were halfway there, which you have to believe or you'll never catch that train, the one carrying saints and sinners and lost souls, the one headed for the land of hope and literary dreams, which is neither here nor there but, rather, in each of us who chase it.

Original Relationships

In Venice some years ago, my wife and I hired a tour guide to shepherd us through the massive collections at the Accademia and the Scuola San Rocco. In the former, he drew our attention to one particular painting that was considered blasphemous at the time because Mary and the infant Jesus were not, as tradition demanded, in the exact center of it. To my untutored eye, this appeared to be a devout depiction of Madonna and child. But it apparently suggested to contemporary viewers that they might not be at the center of everything that mattered. It's unlikely I ever would've seen any of that on my own. Still, it put me in mind of my old grad school professor who argued for what he called "an original relationship" between us and the books we were studying, by which he seemed to mean that we should come to our own conclusions about a poem or story before entertaining the opinions of professional critics. When you're told what to look for, he reasoned, you'll likely find it, and having found it, you'll be less likely to notice what you otherwise might have. What we're talking about here is context—historical, biographical, cultural, religious—that can either enlighten or blind us, depending. I was grateful for our guide in Venice, but after spending two days in his company, Barbara and I began to sense his blind spots. If we expressed interest in a work he'd already decided was uninteresting, he could be downright dismissive. Did we need a second tour guide as a corrective to the first? Or maybe just return to the exhibits by ourselves in the hopes of arriving at our own conclusions?

In *The Lonely City,* Olivia Laing addresses the issue of context in a chapter on Edward Hopper, whose paintings had for a long time been of enormous personal and aesthetic importance to her, a zeal that was tarnished by reading his wife's unpublished diaries, which reveal that Hopper did everything in his power to stifle Jo's artistic career. "The revelation of how violently he worked to suppress her," Laing says, "isn't easy to square . . . with the image of the suited man in his polished shoes, his stately reticence, his immense reserve." Context that we cannot square with belief has a way of quickly becoming toxic, because once we know something, it's impossible to *un*know it or talk ourselves out of it. We understand, intellectually, that great artists are not always good people, but we still want them to be and somehow manage to feel betrayed when they aren't.

I raise this issue because I was in graduate school, trying to become a writer myself, when I first read Andre Dubus, and my relationship to his stories was largely "original" in the sense that I knew very little about him. That said, I did bring a fair amount of personal context to his stories. A lapsed Catholic, I'd been an altar boy for many years and was belatedly discovering that even though I'd successfully flushed most Catholic doctrine from my system, the vocabulary of my former faith—*sin, redemption, grace*—obstinately remained. I admired how seriously Dubus allowed matters of faith to occupy the thematic center of his fiction, like those Renaissance paintings of Madonna and child in Venice. Reading him, I even allowed myself to wonder whether my decision to quit the church had been precipitous, because in truth I missed how warm the church of my youth had been in winter, how cool and dry in summer. The smell of incense, the gentle tinkling of the bell at communion, the sense of an entire community quietly humble in the face of mystery—these were the very elements of faith that Luke Ripley extols in Dubus's "A Father's Story," soothing rituals that nonbelievers throw out with the doctrinal bath water. I probably also sensed that such rituals were not so different from the ones writers use to summon the literary muse; most of us have a favorite time of day to work, a favorite chair to sit in, our favorite pens and writing tablets, favorite coffee cups—objects and habits that help us enter that mysterious world we can never possess but rather are possessed by, to which we gladly surrender ourselves, a state of consciousness that Dubus insisted has less to do with thought than instinct and, yes, feeling. When I first read the stories newly collected in *The Winter Father,* I was also struck by their brave, uncompromising honesty. I recognized in Dubus's plain, simple diction his debt to Hemingway, whose style I, like just about every aspiring young male writer, had admired and flirted with during my long apprenticeship, hoping that I might discover in such plain speech an honesty I feared my own stories lacked.

Later, after actually becoming a writer, I periodically returned to my favorite Dubus stories ("Killings," "Townies," "The Pretty Girl," "A Father's Story"), finding in them other things to admire, though by then my relationship to his fiction was no longer quite so "original." Over the years I'd crossed paths with writers who'd known Dubus well and who provided additional context. He was by all accounts a brilliant, generous teacher who had, alas, an unfortunate habit of taking as lovers his more attractive female undergraduate students. As a father of daughters, I had to squint at this behavior, to remind myself that he was of a different generation and that not so long ago such behavior was common and tolerated, perhaps even impressive. If he wasn't perfect, well, neither was I. What mattered, I told myself, was the stories, and these I still loved. Which was why, when I heard of the terrible highway accident that put Dubus in a wheelchair for the rest of his life, I grieved, and grieved again a decade later when I heard he had died.

But at that point I had not met and become fast friends with his son, Andre Dubus III. It never occurred to me that reading my friend's heartbreaking memoir, *Townie*, might radically alter my perception of "Townies" and the rest of his father's fiction.

My friend Andre tells a hilarious story about the genesis of *Townie*. At a Little League baseball game, he saw a coach loudly berating the kids on his team. Appalled, Andre decided he would himself coach the following year, thereby protecting his sons, who would be old enough to play, and the other kids on the team from such abuse. He would make sure they concentrated on the fun of the game and the rules of good sportsmanship. The problem was that these were the only rules with which Andre was familiar. With his mother and his siblings, he'd grown up in Newburyport and Haverhill in grinding poverty. Not only had he never played baseball, he'd never even watched it on TV, which meant he was ignorant not only of the rules as they applied to professionals but also of how those were modified for kids. As a result, his coaching was unique: he yelled "Run!" to kids on base when they weren't allowed to and demanded they remain at bat until they were able to at least make contact with the ball. The kids he was coaching hilariously had to explain to him it's one, two, three strikes you're out at the old ball game.

Despite *Townie*'s terrifying description of the poverty and violence of Andre's adolescence, the memoir also contains a loving portrait of his famous writer-father, who, at the time, was living just across the river in Bradford, where he taught creative writing at Bradford College and wrote most of the stories contained in this volume. Baseball plays an important role in many of them. The Red Sox are frequently on the television above the bar at Timmy's, the ubiquitous neighborhood tavern, as well as on TVs at the beachfront New Hampshire restaurants just over the Massachusetts line. Several stories feature seemingly autobiographical protagonists who escape their fictional Haverhill/Bradford with their student girlfriends by driving to Boston and taking in a game at Fenway Park. One story, "The Pitcher," showcases the kind of granular detail about the sport that no casual fan would possess. In still other stories, baseball, a sport steeped (like Catholicism) in soothing ritual, actually plays a role in offsetting the toxic effects of the Vietnam War, which often serves as a narrative backdrop. All of which begs an obvious question: If the author felt so strongly about the sport, how is it possible he conveyed none of this to his son? And asking that question opened the door to others. How was it possible this father, who saw his children most weekends, could be so blind to the poverty they and their mother were living in? How could he look at the boy who bore his name and not see that he was constantly being bullied on the streets of then ungentrified Newburyport, that he lived in a state of constant terror and deprivation? How could he feel so little for the woman who'd borne his children and now, as a single mother lacking the necessary resources to raise them, had thrown up her hands in defeat?

Unable to square this new context with my "original" admiration, I found myself rereading these stories with a sinking and, yes, ungenerous heart. When the little boy in "The Winter Father" chases his departing dad's car down the street, crying "You bum! You bum!," I saw not a fictional character but my friend and found myself wholeheartedly concurring with the boy. When the divorced fathers in other stories lamented not being able to pull up stakes and move to Boston because that would mean abandoning their children, I smelled hypocrisy, and in the more Catholic stories, where the protagonists use original sin—man's fallen nature—to excuse shameful, selfish, repetitive behaviors they make no real effort to change, I sniffed it again. If this weren't bad enough, my growing disaffection even altered my assessment of the elder Dubus's style and voice, in particular his debt to Hemingway. When one character suggests to his young girlfriend that they go to Boston, "to Casa Romero and have one hell of a dinner," I cringed, and cringed again every time one of Dubus's tough guys descended into the sort of macho, romantic self-pity for which Hemingway males are so justly famous. Here, I told myself, is a derivative writer who, even in midcareer, is unable to transcend his literary influences. In "Finding a Girl in America," when Hank Allison rhapsodizes about writing as salvation (a soliloquy I'd found thrilling in my late twenties), I winced, and when he describes himself as "an average 260 hitting writer," I saw this as honest, accurate authorial self-evaluation. Just that quickly I'd come to see a man I'd once considered a paragon of honesty as fundamentally *dis-*honest. Having saved it for last, I started rereading "A Father's Story" and had to put it down, afraid that it too might have been contaminated by time and context.

And what did all this portend for the introduction (yes, this one) that I'd agreed to write? The choice I seemed to be faced with was writing something dishonest myself or telling the truth and in so doing risk undermining the reputation of a writer whose work I'd once revered, a betrayal that would not only sadden and anger his many loyal readers but also jeopardize my friendship with his son, who believes—and Andre's been very clear about this—that his father was one of our very finest storytellers. And in writing *Townie*, he made something else clear: if there was anything to forgive his father for, he'd done it long ago.

What, then, does one do with unwanted context? Rattled by Jo Hopper's journal entries about her husband's efforts to ruin her career, Olivia Laing realized that the lens she'd been using to view Hopper had become fogged, her affection for his work undermined. And yet in the end his paintings weren't ruined for her. Why? Unfortunately, her chapter on Hopper doesn't answer that question directly, but it's not impossible to make an educated guess. After all, Hopper was—context be damned—such an undeniably great painter, an artist who painted the truth as he saw it. But I suspected there was more to it and that the *more* was personal. Laing, who at the time was terribly lonely, found Hopper's paintings "consoling" and, as she put it, a kind of "antidote" to her own dark emotional state.

And so, not long after reading these stories and judging their author harshly, I went back to work and was determined not just to give the stories a more sympathetic reading but also to examine my earlier visceral reaction against them, which was already beginning to feel unfair.

Best to begin, I reasoned, with those matters least likely to raise such troublesome contextual issues as friendship and the temptation to read fiction as autobiography, by focusing instead on style, voice and literary influence. Okay, sure, the debt to Hemingway was undeniable, the sparseness of style and diction, especially in dialogue. But there were other less obvious influences too, like Faulkner, whose style is lush, expansive and, well, Southern. We think of Dubus as a New England writer because that's where he spent most of his writing life and set the majority of his stories, but he grew up in Louisiana and the South is ambiently present in his fiction, much as Catholicism is in my own. Dubus's debt to Faulkner, though, has less to do with style than inclination and instinct, a willingness—even a *need*—to burrow deep into the consciousness of characters who, unlike their creator, are too shy or inarticulate or uneducated or lacking in self-awareness to speak for themselves and to give such people a voice. Take, for instance, the title character of "Anna." In the story's opening paragraphs, long before we learn that she and her boyfriend, Wayne, will rob a store, Anna Griffin is revealed to us not in terms of what she has, but rather of what she lacks. A cashier at the Sunnycorner market, she envies the put-together women who work at the nearby bank and wile away their lunch hours thumbing through the store's magazines. These women don't possess *something* Anna lacks; they possess *everything* she lacks. Her poverty becomes even more clear after the robbery when she and Wayne go shopping at the mall, where they buy many of the things they've longed for (and which the women from the bank no doubt have): a color TV, a record player, a vacuum cleaner. The story's brilliance lies in the fact that finally owning these treasures doesn't diminish Anna's sense of penury but deepens it by bringing home to her just how much there is in the world to want; their purchases barely scratch the surface. The most heartbreaking detail here is the vacuum cleaner, whose cord is longer than it needs to be to clean their tiny apartment. Without being able to articulate it, Anna discovers that their new material wealth doesn't really address the root cause of their poverty. When she confesses to a man at Timmy's that what she'd really like is to tend bar there, his response—"you'd be good at it"—haunts her long after their mall purchases have been unpacked. Her deepest destitution resides in her fear that she'll never be good at anything, never be worthy of what others just assume is their due. It's a revelation worthy of Chekhov, a writer Dubus often taught and clearly revered. Many of his best stories contain this kind of Chekhovian "pivot."

Take "The Pretty Girl." Here Raymond Yarborough isn't so much inarticulate as baffled. The story's two distinct narrative points of view provide a dramatic contrast between how Ray sees himself and how the world sees him. Much of the story's tension derives from the refusal of these two narratives to ever really align. To his ex-wife, Polly, and her cop father, Ray is simply crazy and violent, an unhinged thug. Seen through his own eyes, he appears not so much unhinged as confused. He might not understand—himself, his wife, the larger world—but he desperately wants to. "I never know how I feel until I hold that steel," he informs us in the story's haunting first line, and as his narrative unfolds, the reader is struck by his honesty and, at times, even generosity. He tenders all sorts of information about himself, much of it intimate, some of it damning, though that's not how he sees it. And while he isn't a gifted thinker, he does possess a surprising moral imagination. For a man who often doesn't know how he himself feels, he has no trouble imagining how Polly's father must feel after he terrorizes her, and given the opportunity to hurt the man (who has come to hurt him), he demurs.

The real tragedy of Raymond's life seems to be that his experiences seldom lead to genuine understanding, and so the more he tries to explain himself—who he is and why he does what he does—the more bewildered he appears. He's unable, for instance, to make the connection between the steel he refers to in the opening line (the bar of his weight-lifting rig) and the hunting knife he uses to terrorize Polly. Nor does he suspect, as many readers will, that his propensity for violence has something to do with the Vietnam War, which claimed his brother, Kingsley. Indeed, it's thinking about Kingsley—imagining his older brother crawling through the jungle in the moments before he trips the land mine—that leads to his decision to assault Polly's new lover and once again terrify her by setting a fire outside the camp in New Hampshire where she's hiding. Despite being a large man ("It helps in this world to be big," he admits), Raymond seems almost childlike, bewildered that his brother's no longer around to go hunting and fishing and drinking with him. In fact, in the story's climactic scene we understand that Raymond's most lethal characteristic might well be his innocence. He simply doesn't understand why Polly doesn't love him anymore. "What did I do?" he asks her, because so far as he can tell that he raped her at knifepoint is evidence of his depth of feeling, proof of his undying love.

The larger point here is that noting a writer's influences isn't the same as suggesting he lacks originality—as I had done earlier by focusing on Dubus's stylistic debt to Hemingway and ignoring other writers who were equally important to him. Nor should any writer's influences obscure the new uses he puts them to, because Hemingway, Faulkner and Chekhov aside, Dubus's stories feel as fresh today as they did when I first read them three decades ago. One reason is the delight he takes in wrong-footing readers by playing off their genre expectations. Conventional robbery stories, for example, are almost always concerned with whether the thieves will get caught; if they get away with it, the reader usually breathes a sigh of relief. Here it's the exact opposite. Dubus couldn't care less whether Anna and Wayne get caught, because *not* getting caught actually deepens their predicament. Similarly, what initially seems to be the story of a murdered college girl, "Townies," turns out not to be about her at all but rather the unexpected link between the campus cop who finds her body and the boy who kills her, both of whom have been excluded from the privileged girl's world by virtue of their class. Key to conventional stories are clear conflicts that get established early in the narrative so the reader feels oriented and the drama can be heightened. By contrast, Dubus's conflicts are often revealed late in the overall scheme of things and sometimes resolved mere moments later, because he doesn't much care whether we feel oriented or not. He's not here to offer comfort, only truth.

And what truth is that, exactly? I suspect it's the same one Thomas Hardy insisted we grasp nearly a century earlier—that is, just how small and powerless we are against the forces aligned against us. We read Dubus's stories the same way we read *Jude the Obscure*, not to find out what happens next but rather to watch our deepest fears—about ourselves and a brutal, uncaring world—being realized. Dubus's adulterers—adultery is for him the most common and lethal of sins—know not only that what they're doing is wrong but also that it will trail harsh consequences. They're simply unable to repress their desires or even to act in their own self-interest. In "Killings," Frank, the main character's beloved son, knows that his love for another man's wife is dangerous, but love easily trumps both reason and morality. And when Frank's murderer escapes justice to walk the streets of their small town, the young man's father, Matt, has little choice (as he sees it) except to set in motion a murderous plan to put things right. Though readers hope against hope that Matt's lifetime of decency will prevail in the end, they also know better. Fate rules here, making a mockery of both free will and chance. Worse, as readers we are made to feel complicit, judging neither father nor son (or even Raymond Yarborough, for that matter, who speaks of Polly as his addiction, something he has no control over), for these men are as God made them. This is the bad news Dubus feels compelled to share with us: that we are, alas, unequal to many of the most important tasks life sets before us. We are too small and the world too large.

I've not said much about "A Father's Story" to this point, but the time has now come, and I won't mince words. It's one of the finest stories ever written by an American. Any fears I might've had about context diminishing my regard for it did not survive rereading the first page. Art is, after all, its own best defense, although it's probably worth pointing out that in this story, context actually worked powerfully in the writer's favor, for I am, as I said earlier, a father of daughters, a man who would without hesitation do what Luke Ripley does on that dark rural road, and for the same reasons. The story's genius resides in its first-person narrator, whose voice is so powerful, so hypnotizing, so haunting that the reader either forgets or doesn't really care that for three-quarters of the story nothing happens. We're offered no dramatic hook, no clear conflict, no begged question to keep us turning pages. Dubus simply talks to us through Luke, without gimmicks or props, as if our interest in a "big-gutted, gray-haired guy, drinking tea and staring out at the dark woods across the road, listening to a grieving soprano" were a foregone conclusion. As if the unvarying, dogged routine of Luke's everyday life and the crushing loneliness he feels after his wife leaves him were a time-honored, sure-fire method of capturing and holding a reader's attention. As if this old fart's leisurely musings on God and fishing and hunting and baseball and marriage were all any reader had a right to expect from fiction. Because come on, by all rights this story has no business working. By the time something dramatic finally *does* happen, the reader is actually surprised, having come to terms with the possibility—no, probability—that if anything were going to happen, it would have already.

And then, almost before we know it, the story is over, its conclusion as rich and satisfying as anything in contemporary fiction, leaving us to marvel at the alchemy by which the narrative's base metal has been spun into pure gold. What the author has crafted, we realize, is a one-trick story, but this trick is, finally, the only one that really matters. He has made us care. About a big-gutted guy who talks to God because there's nobody else around. Luke Ripley has been instructed, as most of us have, to love God more than the world he gave us, a world that contains our wives and lovers, our sons and daughters, our good work, our pain and loss and struggle. What Luke wants God to understand is that this simply isn't possible. Not for him. Probably not for any of us. I was in my twenties and not yet a father when I first read the story, and at the end when Luke makes his peace with the God he believes he's disappointed, I wept. Thirty some years later—just three weeks ago—I reread it and wept again, for the author I'd once loved and now loved again, for his son and my friend, and, yes, for my own father, who was absent during my young life much as Andre's was. Which is probably why, I now understand, I briefly flirted with disdain and self-righteous disregard for a truly great writer. Because years earlier I'd done exactly what my friend Andre did. I forgave my wayward father. Did so, moreover, for the pleasure of his company and because I could easily imagine doing the exact wrong thing one day myself and then wanting forgiveness for it. I thought I'd forgiven my father completely and without reservation, but apparently not. Some residual resentment apparently remained, and so, without even realizing what I was doing, I offloaded it onto a convenient surrogate.

Edward Hopper once remarked that in all of his paintings, including *Nighthawks,* he was really just trying to paint himself. Maybe that's what all artists and writers do, whether they're aware of it or not. We offer ourselves. *Here I am,* we say, not fully comprehending the nature or value of the offering, only that it's all we have to give.

How Could I?

Denver was the very first stop on my *Empire Falls* book tour back in 2001. At the Tattered Cover store, I read the novel's funniest set piece: young Miles Roby's driving lesson. A good crowd was on hand, and after the reading, there was a long signing line at the end of which stood a woman clutching an advance reader's edition of the book. She'd been a fan for a long time, she told me, her voice quivering with suppressed rage, and what she wanted me to explain was: *How could I?* How could I trade on the grief and loss of people like her for money? She was—it finally dawned on me—from nearby Littleton, a community devastated by the school shooting at Columbine High School two years earlier.

As it happens, the writing of *Empire Falls* had almost nothing to do with Columbine. By 1999, when that tragedy occurred, I had already completed a draft of the novel, which then took a year to revise and another to come out in print. I suppose I might've explained this timeline to my accuser, but to what purpose? She might have been mistaken about the particulars, but in essence she was correct. The school shooting in my book *was* based on a real-life event—the shooting at Heath High School in Paducah, Kentucky, which happened in 1997. The shooter there, like the one in my novel, had been utterly friendless and endlessly bullied because he didn't fit in. So the woman's question—*How could I?*—pertained.

The problem is that for the novelist the opposite question—*How could I* not?—also pertains. Yes, I was thinking about the Paducah shooting when I wrote the book, but its emotional inspiration was a crushing anxiety I was then feeling for the safety of my own daughters, who, when I began the novel, were in middle school and high school, respectively, still girls but approaching young womanhood. To their mother and me, it seemed like only yesterday that they both were open books who freely shared their lives with us over dinner every evening. All that started to change in middle school, where social currency is made and spent and where cruelty and fear become daily facts of life. Suddenly our daughters had private lives. They were entitled to these, of course, but if real danger lurked in the town where we lived, as it had in Paducah, how would I know?

One afternoon my wife and I went to a dress rehearsal of a school play in which our younger daughter had a part. The entire middle school was let out of class to attend. No surprise, they were a rowdy bunch. One kid in particular drew my attention because he sat rigidly still, his face a frozen mask, not engaging with anyone around him, despite the fact that boys in nearby rows were calling him names and hitting him in the back of the head with wadded-up balls of paper and anything else they could lay their hands on. No teacher or other student came to his defense. He just sat there and took it, waiting, unless I was mistaken, for it all to be over, for the relentless torment that was his life to cease. And in that moment this boy, about whom I knew nothing beyond what I'd witnessed, merged in my imagination with the Paducah shooter, now in my daughter's school, perhaps in her class. Over the next four years, as I wrote and revised the novel, that composite boy was my constant companion. Each day became an exercise in magical thinking: if I could face the worst of my fears on the page, maybe I'd be spared in real life. I didn't *want* to write the story, but how could I not?

Looking back on *Empire Falls*—both the novel and the fine HBO miniseries made from it—and trying to imagine how one would tell this story today, I'm most struck by how innocent we all were. Though the book's shooting was foreshadowed, it still came as a profound shock to most readers, who, based on my earlier work, had no reason to expect anything of the sort from me. By the time the miniseries came out in 2005, the novel had won a Pulitzer Prize and people knew what the story was about, but the shock still hadn't worn off; and the director Fred Schepisi's muted, tasteful treatment of the material, which focused more on the run-up and the aftermath than the shooting itself, made that scene even more powerful. Suffice to say that in 2018 the possibility of surprise is long gone.

So how *would* one go about writing a novel that contained a school shooting today? Of course, several have been published since I wrote mine, including Lionel Shriver's *We Need to Talk About Kevin* (2003), Jim Shepard's *Project X* (2004) and Jodi Picoult's *Nineteen Minutes* (2007), as well as, earlier this year, Tom McAllister's *How to Be Safe* and Elise Juska's *If We Had Known*. But I doubt any novelist could write one now that ends the way mine did. After the shooting, which Miles's daughter, Tick, narrowly escapes, Miles feels a single imperative: to protect his child at all costs. To that end, without consulting his ex-wife, he spirits Tick away to a place where she'll be safe and he can help her to mend. In the final scene, a hard-won, qualified optimism is achieved through one of the book's running gags. Miles's car has a glove box with a faulty latch so that every time he goes over a bump the door pops open, which it does one last time when Miles and Tick—together with his father, Max—head back home to Empire Falls.

"You never got that fixed?" Max asks. "I don't think it can be," Miles tells him. "Don't be an idiot," his father replies. "*Anything* can be fixed." Which leaves the reader to ponder the inherent disconnect between this scene and the tragedy looming behind it. Tick has fought hard to pull herself back from the abyss, and we share her father's pride in her recovery. Maybe she'll be okay. But what of the other children, those who were slaughtered? What's the fix for them and their grieving parents? I suspect that's what the woman from Littleton really wanted me to explain. How does my novel help *them*?

And yet it's novels we turn to for a deeper understanding of life than we get from politicians and others with ideological axes to grind, which is why some other writer (probably thinking, *How can I not?*) is no doubt at work on one that centers on a school shooting. Every day she sets about her horrifying task, trying to imagine, *What if one of the dead kids in Parkland was mine? Could I go on? What would my mission in life become after life as I knew it ceased to exist?* Questions like these drive novelists, not because we have answers, but because we don't. All we have is moral imagination, which, over time, can help heal wounds but also has a nasty habit of opening them, as *Empire Falls* did and continues to do.

My heart goes out to whoever is writing that novel today because the task is even tougher now, made more complicated by the fact that such tragedies have become commonplace. We've become less tethered to reality. Though grief and loss are all around us, we prefer to experience them in the form of Avengers movies. And any novel being written today that contains a school shooting will have to take into account a shocking truth—that Miles Roby's fatherly imperative, to protect his child whatever the cost, is not shared across the board in America. As a nation, we have *not* decided that our children are more important than our guns, and any new novel on the subject will have to address that tectonic shift. We've changed. Our nation has changed. A 2018 *Empire Falls* would have to be set in a tribal America that has stopped listening, that might have little interest in a novelist's musings. Even more dispiritingly, it's also an America that has mostly lost our previous generations' faith that things both large and small can be fixed.

These days, the cautious optimism I've lived by, as a novelist and a man, feels strained to the breaking point. And yet, while I don't expect much from our elected leaders (does anybody?), I'm not entirely without hope. That woman who confronted me in Denver? She could've risen to her feet as I started toward the podium and shouted "How *could* you?" before I could even begin. Instead, suffering, she sat patiently while I read the story of young Miles Roby's disastrous driving lesson and while others in the audience, who were not suffering, laughed boisterously. How kind that was. Kindness and moral imagination. We must put our trust in these. And in the fact that they never go completely out of fashion.

Acknowledgments

In addition to my agents, editors, publishers and publicists (home and abroad), who make me appear smarter and more talented than I am with each and every book, I owe special thanks here to Tim Abrahms, Jenny Boylan, Rodney Jones, Phyllis Gottung, Fred Schepisi, David France, Ann Patchett and my long-ago mentor, Bob Downs. And, God help me, there are probably others whose contributions I've somehow managed to forget. Catch you next time.

To Barbara, Emily and Kate: well, I just wouldn't know where to begin.